To Thedore A. Distler

With appreciation of
of a helpful visit,
6/16-17/64, and an
address that will
have a lasting effect
at Southwestern.

Peyton Rhodes

Southwestern at Memphis

Southwestern at Memphis

1848   1948

by

WALLER RAYMOND COOPER

Professor of History, Southwestern at Memphis

John Knox Press

RICHMOND · VIRGINIA

To

President and Mrs. Charles E. Diehl

SOUTHWESTERN IS EVER GRATEFUL TO THEM FOR THEIR
LOYALTY AND DEVOTION

*The publication of "Southwestern: 1848-1948"
has been unavoidably delayed until 1949. The
account of the selection by the Board of Directors of a successor to President Diehl and of
the Centennial Celebration could not be given
in the story of the First Hundred Years.*

🏺 Contents

🙚 Foreword

As SOUTHWESTERN at Memphis completes its first century, it is appropriate that this history should be published and that its author should be precisely the person who was chosen to write it. Professor Cooper is not only the Chairman of the Department of History at Southwestern and a lifelong student of Southern history; he is also that member of the faculty who, with the exception of President Diehl, has been most closely connected with the development of the college during the last twenty-five years. Hundreds of alumni, of whom I am one, cannot recall their student days without remembering with gratitude and pleasure the studies and the personal associations they enjoyed with Professor Cooper: studies and associations that have enriched the lives of all of us.

The story that Professor Cooper has to tell is important, for it is a segment of the story of the South and of Southern education since the tragic days of the War Between the States. Before hostilities began in 1861, the Masonic College from which Southwestern takes its origin had become an instrument in the educational program of a Presbyterian Church that knew no sectional division and that, since before the Revolution, had established schools and colleges in the Middle Colonies, in Virginia, and along the expanding western frontier. When the war ended, what remained of the college, both in physical equipment and in educational ideals, was the possession of a sectional Church, hampered by poverty and by the intellectual isolationism that characterized Southern life in the decades that immediately followed Reconstruction.

The plans of the founders of Southwestern Presbyterian University had been bold, vigorous, and enlightened. That they could not be carried out fully at Clarksville was due to the very conditions of Southern life that war and defeat created. The history of the college until its removal to Memphis in 1925 is, at first glance, the depressing chronicle of failure: failure due to economic distress, to recurring panics, and to a tendency toward obscurantism in the Church itself.

But it would be an error to read the history of those decades merely as a record of failure. The handicaps under which the college operated can be explained by "natural" causes: natural both in the theological and in the human meaning of that word. What cannot be so explained is its success in surviving at all. This was attributable to the remarkable vitality of the institution, a vitality that bespoke the faith and confidence of its faculty and Board of Directors. Those men possessed courage and vision that were more than natural and that heartened them to carry on as best they could the work to which they were committed, even when common sense must have insisted that the cause was hopeless.

It is to those men, devout Christians and devoted teachers, that Southwestern is indebted for its survival during a period in which a shade less of conviction and self-sacrifice might have proved fatal. It was they who kept alive the dream of a great college of liberal arts which would serve not only the Church but the South. They did their work so faithfully that in 1917 there was in existence a Southwestern Presbyterian University for President Diehl to take over. It is difficult to think of anything more typically Southern than this achievement by a small group, not known outside their own community, unaided by funds from Northern foundations, but determined to work as individuals in the rebuilding of the cultural life of their area. It is easy to fasten one's attention on the shortcomings of the Clarksville period, but it is more invigorating and certainly more just to remember gratefully those quiet men who saw to it that the light that Dr. Palmer and others had lighted did not go out.

It is right that President Diehl should be the protagonist of the latter part of Professor Cooper's story. He inherited the college when it had reached its nadir and when the first World War seemed to threaten its very existence. But he inherited also the fine ideals of the founders, and to these he has remained faithful. His achievements illustrate finely and poignantly the old "romantic" conception of history, which is unhappily alien to contemporary thought: the idea that history is the lengthened shadow of great men. Carlyle and Emerson, one feels certain, would know how to evaluate him.

Southwestern as we know it today with its fine buildings, its broad curriculum, its liberal tone, its excellent library, its distinguished faculty, is primarily his achievement. He would be the first to admit that he has not brought all this about single-handed, but those of us who have known the college intimately during the last quarter of a century are aware of the degree to which Southwestern in 1947 is the creation of its president. A careful reading of this history will make plain how splendidly he has worked to realize the hopes and plans of the men who took over the college from the Masons in a time when external forces were hostile or indifferent to much which they hoped to accomplish.

On his retirement President Diehl will turn over to his successor a college that is stable financially, superbly equipped physically, vigorous intellectually, and respected nationally—a college that has every right to claim the support of the Southern Presbyterian Church, the community in which it exists, and its alumni. What President Diehl has done is great, and like all greatness it is the result of courage, devotion, and self-sacrifice. I am sure that he would ask no better reward for his more than thirty years of tireless effort than that we, the Alumni of Southwestern, should understand aright not only his own accomplishments but also those of his predecessors; and that we should guarantee, through our loyalty and generosity, that his long labors on our behalf should bear their finest fruit in the century that lies ahead.

SAMUEL HOLT MONK, '22

Minneapolis, Minnesota
November 30, 1947

I

Montgomery Academy
and Montgomery Masonic College

For the very beginning of Southwestern we must go back to that most interesting period in Tennessee history, the age of "King Andrew"; and to Clarksville, on the Cumberland, where in the turbulent eighteen-thirties a male academy or "log college" was established, which in the following decade developed into the Montgomery Masonic College, the predecessor of Stewart College and the Southwestern Presbyterian University.

It was in 1829 that the rough and ready Andrew Jackson, that idol of the western pioneers, overrode all opposition and became the President of the United States. His own Nashville at this time was little more than a typical frontier village, while Clarksville, the second town in age and importance on the Cumberland, was still very much the whiskey-drinking, gun-toting, pioneer community it had been at the very beginning of the century.

The white population in Clarksville in 1829 amounted altogether to two hundred and fifty souls. This number included sixty-five unmarried men and eight unmarried women. These men and women had little time to think of schools, even if they had been greatly interested in formal education. There were but fifty-six buildings of any description in the town. There was not a resident minister of the Gospel in the place, no church building, and only nine professing Christians of different creeds. "John Barleycorn ruled the hour. He was in every home; in the pockets of the multitude; and all business houses kept whiskey in a conspicuous place for the free use of their respective customers." Since there was no town hall, the office of the mayor was in the street, and the official papers were carried around "in the crown of his Honor's hat."

There was, however, a Masonic Hall, and the members of the Masonic Order seem to have accepted the responsibility of keeping alive whatever interest in education and religion the pioneer Scotch-Irish settlers brought with them from their Carolina and Virginia homes. It was in the Masonic Hall that the few Presbyterians met for occasional services long before they had a church, a pastor, or even a stated supply.

It was the Masonic Order which was chiefly interested in establishing Clarksville Academy, better known as Montgomery Academy, on what was then the outskirts of town, and on the spot which later became the site of the Southwestern Presbyterian University. This academy naturally would be modeled on the famous "log colleges" of the Carolinas, where some, at least, of the Clarksville pioneers had received their early training. The hours were long—from sunup to sundown; the work was hard and the discipline severe.

A new building seems to have been completed in 1837, and the Reverend Consider Parish, a Presbyterian minister and former professor at the University of Nashville, was placed in charge of the Academy. James Grant, editor of the Clarksville *Chronicle* when the Civil War began, was one of his pupils in that year. According to Grant, Professor Consider "was decidedly a considerable teacher. If a pupil violated the slightest regulation, old Consider took it under prompt consideration, and after considering a considerable time, he would give the offender a most considerable thrashing in consideration of his failure to consider rightly what he should have carefully considered."

Reading, writing, arithmetic, English grammar, geography, together with Latin and Greek, composed the curriculum of the Academy. The preacher schoolmasters were interested particularly in teaching their students Latin and Greek. "Thoroughness" was their motto, and their object seems to have been to allow no boy of promise to leave their school without knowing well what he knew at all. For the boy who was eager to learn, "it was Latin in the morning and Greek in the evening, and Latin and Greek both at night." When tallow candles were a luxury to be used only on

THE CASTLE BUILDING

Erected at Clarksville, Tennessee, in 1849

special occasions, the studying at night had to be done by the light from the big open fireplace. The boy was taught to prepare his lessons for the next day by memorizing a few lines while the blaze from the fireplace was burning high, and then, closing his book, to repeat these lines over and over until he was sure he "had them by heart." He would now again build up a bright blaze until he had committed more lines, and then in the fading light would repeat these over and over, until in this manner the entire lesson was learned.

Strong disciplinary methods were needed to enforce the rigid routine of the school on boys accustomed to the active out-of-door life of the frontier. The Reverend Consider Parish was no exception, it seems, to the schoolmasters of the day who considered it their duty to flog the boys all around at regular intervals whether anything particularly worthy of censure had been done or not. Not only did they believe that to spare the rod would spoil the child, but they were also firmly convinced that "flogging a boy loosened up his hide and enabled him to grow." At any rate, we are told that the Board of Trustees, composed of such well-known citizens as John H. Poston, H. F. Beaumont, W. H. Drane, and Andrew Vance, at the end of his first session "took Professor Consider under their consideration, and considering him not considerate enough decided to employ a more considerate man," and on the ninth of July, 1838, they announced the arrival of Mr. Patterson Fletcher, as Principal, and of Mr. Newton, of Virginia, as Assistant.

Whether or not these two men were "too considerate," we do not know, but at the end of their first session they were replaced by the Reverend Abner W. Kilpatrick. For three years "the old man," as the students called him, ruled with a heavy hand. Then the Board secured Mr. Ed Robb to assist him, and at the same time adopted the following resolutions, in which the Board itself assumed some disciplinary control:

"1. All students entering this school shall be considered as entering for the whole session, and the parent or guardian of such student shall be charged for the entire session unless more than one month has elapsed before the entrance of said pupil. No deduction to be made for absence except in cases of protracted illness.

2. The Library and apparatus shall be under the immediate care of the Principal.

3. As strict subordination is absolutely necessary in all well-governed institutions, therefore: Resolved that the Principal will be sustained by the Trustees in the infliction of corporal punishment upon any student of this institution.

4. When any student shall be refractory, and in defiance of remonstrance, fail or refuse to submit to the rules of the Academy, the Principal shall notify the Trustees thereof, whose duty it shall be to meet at the Academy, investigate the matter, and suspend or expel such student, as the case may require.

5. The Trustees will hold a meeting regularly on the first Friday of each month at 3 o'clock P.M. subject to a fine of fifty cents for non-attendance, which fine it shall be the duty of the Treasurer to collect.

6. At each monthly meeting a committee of three shall be appointed, whose duty it shall be to visit the Academy at least twice every month.

7. All profane, obscene language, quarreling, fighting, and immoral conduct of every kind, are positively prohibited by the rules of this institution.

8. Should any student, by his misconduct, subject himself to suspension or expulsion, no deduction shall be made in the tuition fee of said pupil for the session for which he entered.

9. All internal regulations adopted by the Principal for the government of the school will be sustained by the Trustees.

(Signed) JOHN H. POSTON, *President*, WALTER H. DRANE, P. PRIESTLY, BENJ. WILKINS, JAMES B. REYNOLDS, MORTIMER A. MARTIN, H. F. BEAUMONT, CHARLES R. COOPER, GUSTAVUS A. HENRY, *Trustees*."

STEWART HALL

Erected at Clarksville, Tennessee, in 1878

THE PRESIDENT'S HOME IN CLARKSVILLE

From this time (1840) the Academy increased steadily in reputation and prosperity. The ambition of at least some of the Trustees came to be the development of a university in keeping with the progress of Clarksville itself, which now had become one of the most prosperous towns of the West, with its flourishing tobacco market, its macadamized wharf, and its two profitable banks. The most beautiful of the more than fifty steamboats registered in the Cumberland River trade in 1840 had been christened *The Clarksville* as a compliment to the "Magic City." It was *The Clarksville* which took General Jackson to New Orleans in January, 1840, on his last visit to the scene of his victory. When the boat landed at the Clarksville wharf, every boy from the Academy was there to welcome "Old Hickory." Hundreds of other people were there, too, and the *Chronicle* reported that such wild demonstrations of enthusiasm as were made in honor of the grand old soldier "had never before been recorded."

We can see the effects of the ambition of the Trustees to transform the Academy into a college in the fact that on the retirement of Messrs. Kilpatrick and Robb in 1845, they announced with great enthusiasm that Hollis Russell, of Yale, and T. Langdon Anderson, M.D., would be in charge of the Academy during the ensuing year. It was no doubt felt that these men should be able to teach at the college level, and that soon it would be possible to educate their sons in a Clarksville college without having to send them to Lexington, Lebanon, or Nashville.

It would seem, however, that Professor Russell found that not all the patrons of the Academy felt this need of professors who could teach at the college level. For in a letter written from Clarksville in April, 1846, to his grandfather, the Presbyterian minister then living at Walnut Hills, Ohio, he complains:

"Our School was very seriously injured for the present by the establishment of a rival Gamaliel during my absence last winter. He is a disciple from that School of false prophets at Bethany—that hybrid mount Gerizim of modern times. By the twofold scheme of commencing before my return and thus enabling parents to get rid of their boisterous brats some two weeks earlier than they otherwise could—and secondly putting the tuition at about half price he succeeded in seducing more than forty unfortunate sons of Tennessee fathers. These he congregated in a small shanty in the corner of a woodlot which I liken rather to the groves of Baal Peor than the Academus of Plato. We have at present forty-five—from all the most sensible families (ut fit) in town. Of these about twenty are studying Latin, about a dozen Greek and about a dozen more Philosophy or Chemistry and a few are reciting algebra and geometry. I have also a class in French. One of our students is from New Orleans, another from Illinois. Our rival cannot teach the Classics nor the higher mathematics nor can he really teach the sciences. Yet I suppose he would go through a form that would suffice his patrons just as well as teaching.

"The Trustees and our patrons are very anxious to have us remain. Last week they put into my hands $300 to be expended in apparatus with a promise to add $100 per annum while I should remain. I have written to Philadelphia for a select catalogue of Chemical and Philosophical utensils, intending to have them here as soon as possible. The Trustees have also set to work digging a well on the Academy's premises for our sole benefit and have also made divers repairs about the building and will next erect a laboratory and recitation room for Chemical performances."

On the resignation of Professor Hollis Russell at the close of the session, the Trustees, still anxious to develop the Academy into a college, consulted Dr. Philip Lindsley, the revered President of the University of Nashville, and he strongly recommended William H. Marquess, of Nashville, as the man best fitted for carrying out their plans. Consequently, on the first of March, 1847, Mr. Marquess became Principal of the Academy, and in the following year the change from academy to college was finally brought about.

To accomplish this change the Board realized that it would be necessary to find somewhere strong financial backing. The majority, if not all, of the members of the Board were also members of one of the strongest organizations in the country—the Masonic Order. It was natural, therefore, that these Clarksville Masons, through their own local organization, should attempt to get the Masonic Order of Tennessee interested in their college; and it is not strange that the Masons of Tennessee, representing as they did the leading men of the State, enthusiastically endorsed the idea of a great university, to be known as the Masonic University of Tennessee.

On February 4, 1848, the trustees of Clarksville Academy were authorized by the State Legislature to convey the property of the Academy to the Masonic Lodge of Tennessee. This conveyance was made on condition that the Masonic Order of Tennessee would establish and sustain a first-class college in connection with the Academy. In addition to the gift of the Academy assets (which were described as: "The Academy building, a fine two-story brick house capable of accommodating at least one-hundred students, delightfully situated with beautiful grounds enclosed, valued at $5,000, and the small library and philosophical apparatus, valued at $1,000"), the Clarksville Lodge agreed to raise and contribute at least $15,000 toward the erection of a new college building.

The Grand Lodge promptly elected sixteen trustees for the new institution, including five members of the Clarksville Lodge—H. F. Beaumont, W. C. Crane, G. A. Henry, Thompson Anderson, and C. R. Cooper. W. C. Crane was elected Secretary, and the Board held its first meeting in Clarksville on the fifth of December, 1848, "when it was resolved to proceed at once with the organization of the institution, both in its preparatory and collegiate departments." A competent faculty was soon secured, consisting of the following men: "Richard Nelson Newell, A.M., President and Professor of Ancient Languages, with a salary of $1,200; William A. Forbes, A.M., Professor of Mathematics and Natural Science, with a salary of $1,000; Isadore Guillet, Professor of Modern Languages, with a salary of $600; Reverend A. B. Russell, Assistant Professor of Ancient Languages and Principal of the Preparatory Department, with a salary of $800; J. R. Saltonstall, A.B., Assistant Teacher, with a salary of $800; Reverend J. G. Ward, Assistant Teacher, with a salary of $500."

On account of delays and disappointments the collegiate department was not opened until the first day of January, 1849. The enrollment for the first session, however, was very encouraging, and the Board of Trustees in their first report to the Masonic Lodge of Tennessee could state that "since the first day of January last, when it was opened, there have been admitted to the different departments of the University 105 students, and the number is increasing daily."

The cornerstone of the new building was laid with appropriate ceremonies on February 22, 1849, but before it was completed in June, 1850, the Grand Lodge of Tennessee was no longer the owner of the building nor of the institution for which it had been constructed. The University had been founded in 1848, the year in which the Mexican War had been brought to a close by the Treaty of Guadalupe-Hidalgo. The Tennessee pioneers had taken a leading part in this war, and were greatly disappointed that the United States had not kept all of Mexico. They were embittered by the so-called Wilmot Proviso, an attempt to make the exclusion of slavery "an express and fundamental condition to the acquisition of any territory from the Republic of Mexico by the United States." Their pioneer self-sufficiency and already overdeveloped spirit of sectionalism were greatly increased by the partisan struggles over "Manifest Destiny" and the bitter debates produced by the annexation of California and the Mexican purchase.

It is not surprising, therefore, in such times as these that the attempt to arouse a state-wide interest in education was impossible. Dr. Philip Lindsley, who had endeared himself to Tennesseans by refusing the presidency of Princeton to accept the presidency of the University of Nashville, and who had labored, using all the power and influence of his outstanding reputation and popularity, to build up a "Princeton" for the South, disappointedly exclaimed, "I did once flatter myself that the people of Tennessee would rally round this infant seat of science, and take a just pride in its growth and prosperity. I did suppose that they would cherish an institution of their own, established in their own flourishing metropolis." The spirit of sectionalism, even within the state, was too strong for the great Dr. Lindsley.

Likewise, the Clarksville Masons, in 1848, had found that the Masonic Order of Tennessee, though interested in establishing the Masonic University of Tennessee, was finding it impossible to interest the Masons of the whole state in an institution established in any one section of Tennessee. Each local order had wanted the University placed within its own borders, and now preferred the placing of a small Masonic college within its own section to the establishing of a strong university in any other section than its own. As a result of this policy, many small Masonic colleges, without sufficient funds or patronage, sprang up throughout the state, and the Masonic Order of Tennessee found it impossible to foster the University which it had begun.

The Grand Lodge soon withdrew its support from the University and reconveyed to the trustees of the Clarksville Academy the property which the Lodge had received on condition that it would establish and sustain a first-class college on the property. When, therefore, the Clarksville institution opened in 1850, it was no longer under control of the Grand Lodge of Tennessee but of the local lodge. A charter was secured in 1851 incorporating the institution as Montgomery Masonic College, and the trustees of the old Academy promptly conveyed the property returned by the Grand Lodge to the trustees of Montgomery Masonic College.

W. F. Hopkins served as the first President of the reorganized institution and two, at least, of the first faculty, William A. Forbes, Professor of Mathematics, and William M. Stewart, Professor of Natural Sciences, not only served in turn as President of the Montgomery Masonic College before its change into Stewart College in 1855, but also rendered conspicuous service in the later development of the institution.

One of the first needs of the Masonic College had been a suitable college building. One might think that an inexpensive building without pretense to architectural beauty would have been contemplated by the Trustees in the disturbing days following the Mexican War, but such was not the case. The Masonic leaders were wiser than this. They wanted a building that would fitly express the high ideals of their Order, one that would be famed throughout the West; and in carrying out this purpose they were surprisingly successful.

The well-known architect, G. B. Vannoy of Gallatin, had been employed to design and superintend the construction of the building at the then extravagant cost of $32,000. It is no wonder that this building immediately on its completion in 1850 became the pride of Clarksville. Professor Stewart boasted: "The College Building is located in a beautiful grove of native forest trees near the limits of the Corporation, on a gently elevated, but commanding position, well calculated to attract the eye, and improve the taste, and so remote from the business part of the town as to be well adapted to quietude and study. The edifice is one of the most stately, elegant, capacious and imposing in our country, built in the Elizabethan style of architecture, a fine model of a castellated building"; and the editor of the *Jeffersonian* exclaimed, "What an elegant structure it is! of vast extent; and built in the handsomest style of Elizabethan architecture it arrests the admiring attention of every passer-by, no matter were he from Rome, that city of St. Peter's Cathedral." This "Castle Building" was still the most imposing structure on the campus when Southwestern was finally moved from Clarksville to Memphis in 1925.

One other thing, at least, gave fame to the young Masonic College, and that was the presence on its faculty of the distinguished scientist and philanthropist, William M. Stewart. Professor Stewart was a Philadelphian by birth, but in 1832 had migrated to Tennessee, where superior scientific attainments had enabled him to accumulate a considerable fortune in the iron business. During his busiest years he had found time for a hobby begun in early childhood with the observing and collecting of insects and shellfish, and stimulated by a voyage to the West Indies, where his opportunities for observation were enlarged. Before leaving Philadelphia he had in connection with other associates organized in that city the Academy of Science, which soon became one of the most noted institutions of its kind in America. He was the friend of Matthew Fontaine Maury and was among the first of the scientific men to be employed by the Smithsonian Institute in the elaborate system of observations, extending over the habitable world, which established meteorology as a science of most important practical application. His interest in the success of the college at Clarksville caused him to accept first a professorship and later the Presidency of the Masonic College. His untiring labor and generous financial contributions to the institution enabled it to exist during the period when the intellectual leaders of his state were too absorbed in "Bleeding Kansas," the purchase of Cuba, the Abolition Crusade, and the other stirring political questions of the day, to give much thought to the needs of the Masonic College.

It became necessary, therefore, for President Stewart to look elsewhere for the support of his institution. His disinterested love of the sciences and his enthusiastic interest in the cultural growth of his community had enabled him to press on the college the ideals of honesty and thoroughness. The Presbyterian leaders were particularly impressed, and with the support of the Reverend J. T. Hendrick, pastor of the Clarksville Presbyterian Church, the Synod of Nashville was induced to consider the purchase of the Masonic College as the ideal solution of its need for a Presbyterian college within the borders of the Synod. In 1855, therefore, the buildings, grounds, and other possessions of the Montgomery Masonic College were purchased in the name of the Synod of Nashville; and the name of the college was changed in honor of its distinguished patron and President to that of Stewart College.

Fortunately, the day had not yet arrived when the Presbyterian Church in America would be split into two sections. Thus, when the college at Clarksville came under Presbyterian control in 1855, it became the college of a powerful united Church; a Church famed for its interest in higher education; a Church which not only had established a splendid college at Princeton, but had led the way in fostering educational institutions in every section of the rapidly expanding country.

President Stewart was a Presbyterian elder, steeped in the educational traditions of his Church. He had been reared at Philadelphia, hard by the college at Princeton, and was well aware of the importance of such an educational institution as Princeton to the Church as well as to the State. It would naturally become his great ambition to build, with the support of the Church, his frontier college into a Princeton for the South. The later separation of the Southern Presbyterians from their Northern brethren, and the establishment of a separate Southern Presbyterian Church, was to be a bitter disappointment to him, for it made impossible the fulfillment of his dreams for a Presbyterian college supported by a united Church, able and willing to foster its educational institutions at all costs.

II

Stewart College:
Before the War Between the States

THE FAITH of President Stewart and of the citizens of Clarksville in the success of their college now that it had become the college of the Synod of Nashville, was based on their knowledge that the Presbyterian Church had always been a strong advocate in the field of higher education. As early as 1746, a small group of ministers in the Synod of New York had, in association with the Presbyterian Church, established at Princeton the College of New Jersey, which had played such an important part in the educational history of the early Republic, and soon became known as the "Mother of Colleges."

Such well-known frontier institutions as Washington College at Lexington, Virginia; Hampden-Sydney College at Hampden-Sydney, Virginia; Washington and Jefferson College at Washington, Pennsylvania; Centre College at Danville, Kentucky; Hamilton College at Clinton, New York; Illinois College at Jacksonville, Illinois; Maryville College at Maryville, Tennessee; and Wabash College at Crawfordsville, Indiana, had all been founded by Presbyterians and in close association with the Presbyterian Church. In 1848, the year in which the college at Clarksville was founded, the General Assembly of the Presbyterian Church had declared that colleges were an integral part of the American way of life, and in their widespread relations to the best interests of society were a vitally important part of a complete system of education and demanded the fostering care of the Church. And in 1853 the Assembly's Board of Education had asserted that it was the avowed policy of the Presbyterian Church to sustain institutions of higher learning under her own care. Furthermore, it had long been the boast of the Presbyterian Church that among Presbyterians learning and religion go hand in hand, and that the history of Presbyterianism in any section is largely also an educational history of that region.

As an elder in the Presbyterian Church, President Stewart was well aware of the traditions of his Church, and felt that his faith in the progress of Stewart College under Presbyterian control was altogether justified, as no doubt it would have been had not the unfortunate division into a Northern and a Southern Church been brought about. This separation would necessarily weaken the Church and prove a heavy blow to the educational institutions under its control.

The college at Clarksville opened for its first session as Stewart College, under Presbyterian control, in September, 1855. The faculty was reorganized with a President, four members of the college faculty, and two teachers in the preparatory department. The literary department of the University of Nashville and that of the University of Mississippi at this time had the same number of professors. It was with great enthusiasm, therefore, that President Stewart agreed to continue as President of the newly organized institution with a full faculty, composed of distinguished professors elected by the Board of Trustees but chosen by himself. An attractive catalogue was published proudly announcing President William M. Stewart as Professor of Natural History; William A. Forbes, A.M., as Professor of Mathematics, Natural Philosophy, Astronomy, and Civil Engineering; Lucius G. Marshall, A.M., as Professor of Latin and Greek Languages and Literature; Rev. J. T. Hendrick, D.D., as Professor of Mental and Moral Philosophy and Evidences of Christianity; E. B. Haskins, M.D., as Professor of Chemistry; and R. W. Daniel and Edward Hewitt as Instructors in the Preparatory Department. The catalogue further announced that "the Chemical and Philosophical apparatus are new, complete and of the most recent and improved character. The extensive and elegant Mineralogical and Geological Cabinet of the late Professor Vanuxen of Philadelphia has been added by our President to the previous collection, which together with a complete laboratory, and the numerous Geological and Meteorological drawings, afford the amplest and very best facilities for the study of the natural sciences. . . . With such ample accommodations, complete apparatus, and with a full and able Faculty, the Trustees feel assured that they can offer the best facilities that our country can afford for the acquisition of a complete classical and scientific education."

Two courses of instruction were offered—the four-year prescribed course leading to a degree, and the three-year scientific course "for those students who may not desire to pursue the prescribed course in college." The prescribed course was that offered in practically all of the better colleges of the day, and consisted of a thorough study of Latin, Greek, and Mathematics in the freshman year; Latin, Greek, Mathematics, and Surveying in the sophomore year; Latin, Greek, Natural Philosophy, Mechanics, and Chemistry in the junior year; and Latin, Greek, Mental Philosophy, Logic, Political Economy, Moral Philosophy, Evidences of Christianity, Mineralogy, Astronomy, Meteorology, Geology, and Zoology in the senior year.

In the three-year scientific course the student was required to take Mathematics, Chemistry, Meteorology, and Rhetoric in the first year; Mathematics, Political Economy, Mineralogy, Surveying, Navigation, Natural Philosophy, and Zoology in the second year; and Mental Philosophy, Natural Philosophy, Mathematics, Moral Philosophy, Evidences of Christianity, Geology, and Astronomy in the third year.

All students of the college were required to take part in the "exercises in elocution and composition" each Friday afternoon, and both students and professors were required to assemble in the chapel each morning before beginning the regular duties of the day, for prayers and roll call. Article Third, Section Third, of the rules and regulations printed in the catalogue provided that the hours of study for the collegiate students each day of the week, except Saturday and Sunday, would be as follows:

"Study or recitation from 8 A.M. to 12.
Study or recitation from 2 P.M. to 5 P.M.

Study at home from 7 P.M. to 6 A.M.

On Friday the student shall be in his room by 11 P.M. On Saturday from 8 P.M. to 6 A.M."

The enthusiasm with which President Stewart entered on his work in making Stewart College the pride of Clarksville and the Southwest was soon reflected in the enthusiasm of the members of the Board of Trustees and of the people of Clarksville. Neither the President nor the members of the Board nor the citizens of Clarksville realized, however, the cost of such an institution. So long as men like President Stewart or Dr. Haskins could be found who were able and willing to donate their services to the college and to purchase from their own funds the necessary equipment for the laboratories, the financial support of the Church and community would not be so necessary; but sooner or later a success built on such a financial basis must end, and the lack of an adequate endowment would probably be the downfall of a splendid institution.

President Stewart was the ideal man for giving tone to the frontier college and for establishing ideals of genuine scholarship and of right living among the students. The fact that this grand old man had been able to accumulate a fortune and might have spent his latter years in any way he chose, but that he actually preferred scientific research and the unremunerative life of a teacher, must have had a tremendous influence on every student of Stewart College. Unlike the parents of these boys, President Stewart, the former "Iron King," considered it much more essential for the welfare of Clarksville to establish a thriving college than to secure a railroad connecting the community with the outside world.

This road seems to have been the one interest of the Clarksville business men at the time. Any sacrifice to obtain the railroad connecting Clarksville with Memphis and Nashville was considered none too great, and the need for a college seemed small in comparison. Editor Thomas of the *Chronicle* expressed the idea of the leading citizens in the following editorial: "True we have had our foundries and machine shops, tobacco stemmeries, steam sawmills, planing machines, steam wagon factories, etc., etc., for some time in operation, but we think we hazard nothing in saying that these are but a mere circumstance to what will be when that *Road* is built, and the treasurer says they hope to build in two years, if the subscribers will pay up." But he gives a note of warning against placing the value of the railroad above that of the College when he continues: "We had rather see that Road in operation than to see anything else, short of everybody's being made tremendously rich, and the establishment of a flourishing institution of learning in our midst." And again: "Yet we do not think the interest taken in this matter [financial support of Stewart College] at all commensurate with the importance of the institution to the community in a *moral, intellectual,* or even a *pecuniary* view. . . . In the pressure of various other interests those of education do not receive a due share of our attention. . . . It is a shame and reproach to a wealthy community like Clarksville that it will suffer other localities to take away the palm of competition in this respect." "Our citizens," he continued, "are interested only in business. To be sure, business is a very commendable thing in its place, but mankind owe a higher and nobler duty to their posterity than to accumulate a fortune for them. . . . If we need a Dormitory and Boarding House for our College . . . we are very able to build it: let us go to work in earnest and have it."

President Stewart realized that he was unfitted by inclination and disposition for the aggressive work needed in raising an endowment for the college. His modest, retiring nature and his intense interest in and devotion to his scientific researches made the tasks of his office so burdensome that at the end of two years he handed in his resignation as President of the college, which the Board of Trustees reluctantly accepted on his promise to continue his invaluable services as Professor of Natural Sciences.

During the regime of President Stewart the college in a surprisingly short time had established a reputation for high standards and thorough scholarship. Its scientific equipment compared favorably with that of other frontier colleges at that time. Its faculty was unexcelled in the Southwest but also unpaid. Financial difficulties seemed the one obstacle to permanent success.

Consequently, when the Synod of Nashville met in the Presbyterian Church of Clarksville in October, 1858, the future of Stewart College was its chief concern. The raising of an endowment fund was imperative, and it was essential, therefore, that a new President be selected who would be fitted for this task and at the same time be able to foster the high scholastic and cultural standards established by President Stewart.

After a long and spirited debate and the offering of numerous amendments, the Synod finally adopted unanimously the report of the Committee on Colleges. The resolutions expressed thanks to President Stewart, Professor Forbes, Professor Hendrick, and Professor Haskins for their services gratuitously rendered the college, and regret at the resignation of President Stewart. They further empowered the Trustees to elect a permanent President who should be the agent of the college in the endeavor to procure an endowment of $150,000, all subscriptions to be void unless the sum of $50,000 was secured before January 1, 1861. The Rev. R. B. McMullen, D.D., of Knoxville, was recommended by the Synod for this position, and it was later announced that the Trustees had met and unanimously elected Dr. McMullen as President of Stewart College.

Dr. McMullen, when called to the presidency of the college, was serving as pastor of the First Presbyterian Church of Knoxville. He had been educated at the University of Alabama and at Princeton and after graduation had devoted his time to teaching as well as to preaching. He had come to Knoxville in 1841 from Alabama to accept the Chair of Chemistry in the East Tennessee University (now the University of Tennessee), but after a short time in this position had been persuaded by the Presbyterian congregation to become pastor of their church. This necessitated his resigning as professor at the University, but he remained deeply interested in the educational progress of his Church, and lost no opportunity to advocate the cause of the Presbyterian colleges in the courts of the Church. In recognition of his services to the cause of Christian education,

Washington College conferred on him the degree of Doctor of Divinity in 1855. Realizing the wider opportunities for service in the educational work of the Church which the position at Clarksville would bring him, he did not hesitate to accept the Presidency of Stewart College when this position was offered to him by the Trustees in October, 1858.

Dr. McMullen arrived in Clarksville at the beginning of the new year, and at once announced that he was ready and anxious to "put forth all his energies in the laudable enterprise" of raising a permanent endowment for the college. The plan adopted by the Trustees for this purpose was to secure donations and subscriptions for scholarships; then to invest this endowment fund, and out of the annual accruing interest—not touching the principal—to pay the professors. Any person subscribing $500.00 payable in five equal annual installments would be entitled to send one pupil, from the date of the first payment, to any department of the college "as long as the College endures." The scholarship would be transferable and might be willed like other personal property.

The Trustees, on the arrival of Dr. McMullen, announced that the faculty of Stewart College for the following session would include: the Reverend R. B. McMullen, D.D., President and Professor of Mental and Moral Science, and Evidences of Christianity; W. M. Stewart, A.M., Professor of Natural History; the Reverend A. A. Doak, D.D., Professor of Ancient Languages and Literature; W. A. Forbes, A.M., Professor of Mathematics and Natural Philosophy; the Reverend T. DeLacey Wardlaw, A.M., Professor of English Literature and Criticism; E. B. Haskins, M.D., Professor of Chemistry; the Reverend William Mack, D.D., Professional Lecturer on History; James K. Patterson, Adjunct Professor and Principal of the Preparatory Department. To this list of faculty members was added the following announcement:

"The Trustees beg leave to call attention to the marked ability of the Faculty. They are all agreeable and affable gentlemen of long experience and eminent ability as instructors devoted to their professions, and have proved themselves to be learned, energetic and persevering in their several departments. The Trustees assert with confidence that the Faculty is inferior to none in the whole country, either in learning, ability or professional zeal, and they are determined to make the institution equal to any in the country in point of thoroughness of education and accomplished scholarship."

Such enthusiasm was aroused immediately by President McMullen that in February the editor of the *Chronicle* asserted that anyone who had mingled freely with the citizens of Clarksville during the past month could not fail to notice that the interests and prospects of Stewart College had engrossed a large and prominent share of the conversation during that time. Everyone, he stated, was intensely interested in the endowment, "especially property-holders, heads of families and the traders in the city whose business will be largely increased." He was happy in the belief that the pecuniary difficulties with which the college had had to struggle in the past few years were now completely and forever removed, for already an endowment of $40,000 had been raised in the city alone, with the prospects of obtaining ten to twenty thousand more. "And now," he concluded, "the whole community seems alive in promoting the interests of the College. The certainty of its success is now complete."

This renewed interest of the community in the welfare of the college was reflected in the life of the students. Especially did the enthusiastic support given by the members of the Board of Trustees in every phase of their college life inspire the students with a determination to excel in order that they might win the approval of these men who were not only the leaders in the community, but were also the men to whom the citizens of the whole state were looking for leadership in the critical period of the Kansas-Nebraska Bill, the Dred Scott Decision, and the John Brown Raid. Gustavus A. Henry, the "Eagle Orator of Tennessee," Cave Johnson, the right-hand man of President Polk and his able Postmaster-General, Judge Thomas W. Wisdom, Thomas W. Beaumont, the leading Whig

FACULTY AND STUDENT BODY OF 1886

JOSEPH R. WILSON
Professor of Theology and Homiletics,
1885-92

THOMAS OAKLEY DEADERICK
Professor of Latin and French,
1891-1914

editor of the State, Robert W. Humphreys, hero of the Mexican War, Senator James E. Bailey, Alfred Robb, the brilliant young lawyer, Charles O. Faxon, Editor of the *Jeffersonian,* William P. Hume, of the Planters Bank of Tennessee, and D. N. Kennedy, President of the Northern Bank of Tennessee, were all men of state-wide reputation and some of national reputation and interests, yet were not too busy to take a personal interest in the students of Stewart College, where some of them, at least, had sons in attendance.

Two literary societies were formed among the students—the Washington Irving and the Stewart—and in these centered the social life of the college. The rivalry between the two was intense, and the determination of the members to win the plaudits of their distinguished guests made the joint debates of the societies important events in the social life not only of the college but of the whole community. Rooms were set aside in the college building for the use of both societies, and with the aid of the young ladies of the town, these rooms were most conveniently and attractively arranged. Each society had its own library; and when new books were needed, a pleasant social affair was planned by the students to which the public was invited. The *Chronicle* of April 23, 1858, reported: "The time of the May Supper at Stewart College has been changed by postponement to the 13th in order that the affair may be made more complete and perfect in all respects, but particularly in order that strawberries and cream may enter largely into the list of table luxuries. Everyone who is supposed to indulge in the brightest social festivities, or to aid a worthy enterprise, should be certain to attend the May Supper, for it will be a most elegant entertainment and the proceeds are to be devoted to a very desirable object. Admission tickets can be had for $1.00."

The personal interest of Mr. Alfred Robb, the youngest member of the Board of Trustees, and Mr. William Forbes, Professor of Mathematics, had much to do in forming early traditions at Stewart College. The students said that Mr. Robb "carried his head nearer heaven than any man in the State of Tennessee," for he was nearly seven feet tall. He was a brilliant young lawyer, and greatly interested in the debating and oratorical activities of the students. He realized that if the college would attract the patronage of "foreign students" (in this age of intense sectionalism, all students from beyond the borders of the county were called "foreign"), then there must be provided for their use a college dormitory. So great was his zeal in this matter that at the June meeting of the Board in 1859 he offered to present his valuable lot adjoining the campus to the Trustees if they would undertake to build dormitories thereon. This offer was promptly accepted; each Trustee made a liberal donation for the building, and work on "Robb Hall," the first college dormitory, was soon begun.

Professor Forbes, the close personal friend of Mr. Robb, was also greatly interested in the debates in the society halls, particularly when they dealt with the question of States Rights. He was a Virginian by birth, intensely jealous of any claims of the Federal Government to interfere with the affairs of the State, and ready to advocate secession if the Northern Whigs should refuse to abide by the Compromise of 1850, and should become strong enough to threaten the supremacy of the Democratic party. And it was Professor Forbes who, reading the signs of the times, became interested in "preparedness," organizing the students into a company for military drill; so that when Tennessee, after Fort Sumter, finally decided to cast in her lot with the Confederacy, every student at Stewart College except two, living outside the bounds of the Confederacy, promptly answered the call of his country, and entered the Confederate Army.

This was a stunning blow to the college which had entered on its second year under the leadership of the new President with such brilliant prospects. It could already boast that it was an outstanding college of the growing Southwest. The literary department of the University of Nashville had fallen on evil days since the loss of the revered Dr. Lindsley, and neither the University of the South at Sewanee nor the Vanderbilt University at Nashville was yet in existence. For the first time, Stewart College had become self-supporting under the new regime, and was receiving what seemed in comparison to the indifference of earlier days, the enthusiastic support of both the Presbyterian Synod and the citizens of Clarksville. An outstanding event in the cultural life of Tennessee in 1859 was the inauguration of President McMullen, when ceremonies "commensurate with the importance of the occasion" were held at Clarksville characterized by the enthusiastic participation of the friends and patrons of the college. The widely known Dr. Edgar of Nashville represented the Synod on this occasion and "in glowing periods touched and instructed the patriotism of those present." Alfred Robb, on behalf of the Board of Trustees, "in brief but exceedingly neat and appropriate address," presented the keys of the college to the President. Dr. McMullen's address, "of some fifty minutes in length," was a masterpiece, in which he gave his views as to what education should be, showing that "man in his triune being—body, mind, and soul—should be thoroughly educated." As to Stewart College, he said, "Its teaching shall be *thorough*, its discipline moral, parental (in the true sense of the term), and impartial." He presented many suggestive statistics showing the benefit of and the necessity for Church colleges where the fundamental principles of Christianity are inculcated. Stressing the necessity for institutions of higher learning for the academic training of ministers for the Presbyterian Church, he added: "But how are our ministers to be supplied? Who is to teach and train them? Who will found colleges and sustain professors to train up a ministry in the Presbyterian Church? Will other denominations do it? Are they under obligation to furnish funds and men for our good? . . . Or may we look to the state institutions for the performance of this great and necessary task? Will they supply us with ministers? Nay, verily."

The bright future for the college was the one topic of conversation in Clarksville during the week of the inauguration in December, 1859. For a short time, at any rate, the madman John Brown, and his lawless attack on Harper's Ferry during the past summer, were forgotten. The sacrificial gift of Alfred Robb to the college and the immediate response of the Board of Trustees with money from their own pockets to insure the erection of a dormitory for the use of "foreign" students, the successful campaign for $50,000 raised in Clarksville and Montgomery County alone, the prospects for the success of the campaign for $100,000 for the endowment of the college, the impressive ceremonies connected with the inauguration of President McMullen—these were now the topics of conversation wherever the citizens met.

The larger number of students enrolled at the college during the session of 1859-60, particularly the increase in the number of dormitory students, was tangible evidence of the growing reputation of the institution throughout the Southwest. The Synod of Nashville at its meeting in Tuscumbia, Alabama, enthusiastically resolved to endow two professorships of $20,000 each in Stewart College, one to be called the Edgar professorship, in honor of the beloved Dr. Edgar, of Nashville, and the other to be named in honor of the ladies of the Synod, who asked to be allowed to raise this amount for the endowment of a chair. Almost at once there was a large meeting of the ladies of Clarksville held in the Presbyterian Church and the "Stewart College Ladies Professorship Association" was formed, with Mrs. E. B. Haskins as President; Mrs. A. Robb as Vice-President; Mrs. G. A. Henry, Mrs. W. M. Stewart, Mrs. W. M. Finley, Mrs. T. J. Munford, Mrs. Bryce Stewart, Mrs. W. B. Munford, and Mrs. Joshua Elder, as Directors; Mrs. M. Stacker as Treasurer; and Mrs. G. T. Lewis as Secretary. Plans were made to secure twenty-five subscribers at $20.00 annually for four years; two hundred subscribers at $10.00 annually for four years; and five hundred subscribers at $5.00 annually for four years. The *Chronicle* predicted a grand and immediate success for these plans; "the fact that the ladies have determined to endow a chair is a guaranty for its success, for they never fail a good work."

Dr. McMullen based his great hopes for the growth and future success of the college on his splendid faculty, each of whom was not only a scholar with more than a local reputation in his field, but also a Christian gentleman of the highest type, personally interested in the all-round development of his students. The influence of Professor Stewart and of Professor Forbes has already been noted. James K.

Patterson, the distinguished President of the University of Kentucky from 1869 to 1910, was a young member of Dr. McMullen's faculty. He was greatly impressed by the able men with whom he was associated at Stewart College, and in later life often referred to the delightful companionship of Dr. McMullen, Dr. A. A. Doak, and Dr. T. D. Wardlaw, and to the interest shown by them in their students. Dr. Wardlaw was a graduate of King's College, Belfast, and the Professor of English Literature and Criticism at Stewart College. It seems to have been his custom and delight to invite his students to his home where they read together the classics with a zest before unknown to the students, often concluding the readings with a refreshing "mid-night supper."

In 1858 Dr. McMullen had thought that the future of the college would be secure when the endowment should be fully subscribed. In 1860 this endowment had been assured but there still remained a serious danger threatening the destruction of both endowment and college. It now seemed probable that the Southern States would eventually secede from the Union, and altogether possible that secession might result in a civil war which would surely bring disaster and ruin to the young college.

The national conventions and campaigns of 1860 were of the greatest interest, therefore, to everyone connected with Stewart College. It was with feelings of intense excitement that the faculty and students read on the afternoon of April 25, 1860, the announcement in the *Jeffersonian* that their friend and patron "Alfred Robb, Esq., delegate from this Congressional district to the National Democratic Convention, left here for Charleston on Wednesday evening's train." From this time on, events of national importance tended to place in the background all questions of local concern; and trustees, faculty, and students alike found themselves absorbed in the fate of their country. Yancey's walkout at the Charleston Convention and the split of the Democratic Party into a Northern and a Southern section, the organization of a Union Party with John Bell of Tennessee as its candidate for President, the welding of the Whig and the Republican parties into a sectional party with Lincoln as its candidate for President—all seemed to point to the near end of the Union. The election of Lincoln in November, 1860, made this dreaded event appear almost a certainty.

The Stewart College boys had little time now for their Latin and Greek. Professor Forbes and his military company occupied their thoughts during the day, and the exciting political questions of the hour caused them to neglect their studies at night while they gathered for endless discussions on the possibilities of secession and war.

The length of these discussions and the excitement of the students were greatly increased by the news that South Carolina had seceded from the Union and that a Southern Confederacy had been formed at Montgomery. So intense was their excitement when the news of the bombardment of Fort Sumter was received that all the able-bodied students in Stewart College, under the leadership of Professor Forbes, marched out to the Fair Grounds, where they encamped until Tennessee withdrew from the Union, when Captain Forbes's company became the first in the county to answer the call of the Governor for troops.

III

Stewart College:
During War and Reconstruction

On the outbreak of war, President McMullen was left without students and without a faculty at Stewart College. He did not despair, however, as is shown by this notice which he inserted in the *Jeffersonian* on July 19, 1861:

"When our northern invaders declared war against the South, one of the Professors of the institution and nearly every student who was able to bear arms, promptly enrolled themselves for defense of the South and are now in the army. On the first Monday in September next the exercises of the College will again be resumed. If our soldiers shall not have driven back our oppressors ere that time, most of our elder students will of course not be with us at the commencement of the session, but the younger members can come.

"We earnestly hope that before September our invaders will have received such salutary lessons as will induce them to remove their polluting feet from our sacred soil, so that teachers and pupils may return to their literary and scientific pursuits. But if in this we are disappointed, we will wait till our brethren and fellow-students shall have taught the President and Cabinet to march from Washington in a still more lively double-quick step than they employed in marching to it.

"Discipline—our motto is this—'We act toward every student as Christian gentlemen, and we require them to treat us in like manner.' And we are happy to say that thus far they have nobly complied with our requirements.

"All young men studying for the Ministry in any evangelical denomination will be instructed gratuitously."

Dr. McMullen's fervent hopes that before September "our invaders will have received such salutary lessons as will induce them to remove their polluting feet from our sacred soil, so that teachers and pupils may return to their literary and scientific pursuits" were not realized. Therefore, on September 5, the Trustees met and authorized the President to continue the college if he thought proper on his own responsibility. This he undertook to do in spite of the fact that every former student of the college was in the army and the dormitories were being used as a Confederate hospital. Thirty-six preparatory students enrolled during the first term, but before the end of the term Dr. McMullen moved into the home of Captain W. A. Forbes, turned over all college buildings to the Confederate government, and continued the school in the lecture room of the Presbyterian Church. Even this arrangement proved temporary, for on the fall of Fort Donelson and the occupation of Clarksville by the Federal troops, the school was closed, not to be opened again until after the war had ended.

When the Fourteenth Tennessee Infantry was organized at Clarksville in May, 1861, Professor Forbes was chosen Colonel of the regiment. The company of college boys which he had organized and drilled while still a professor at Stewart College now became a part of this regiment. When, however, in July the Fourteenth Tennessee was ordered to Virginia, the Colonel refused to allow those boys who were unable to obtain the consent of their parents to march off to war with him. Naturally, they were very indignant at the time, but those left behind did not have long to wait, for when Governor Isham G. Harris made a second call for troops in November, they promptly joined the Clarksville company organized by James E. Bailey, a member of the Board of Trustees of Stewart College. On the sixth day of December, 1861, this company left Clarksville on a steamboat for Fort Donelson, "amidst the shouts of the citizens, the waving of the handkerchiefs of the ladies, and the firing of guns from the fort at Red River," and arrived at Fort Donelson that night, where they soon became members of the newly organized Forty-Ninth Tennessee with James E. Bailey as their

Colonel, and another Stewart College trustee, Alfred Robb, as their Lieutenant Colonel.

The fact that so many Clarksville boys were stationed at the fort explains to some extent why Dr. McMullen was forced to close his school when the bombardment at Fort Donelson began. The *Jeffersonian* of February 15 reported: "The excitement here, during the bombardment of Fort Donelson, on Thursday, was intense. The report of the guns could be distinctly heard, and their frequency created the impression that a bloody fight was going on. . . . From every portion of this and adjoining counties people poured in to catch the first inkling of this news. . . . There has been a perfect rush of people . . . seeking passage to Fort Donelson. Fathers and brothers eager for a fight or to look after the safety of their kinsmen in the regiments there. Many got off—some on steamboats and some by land. . . . As Pillow has ordered the hospitals here to be made ready for those who may be wounded at Fort Donelson, it is inferred that he does not intend that Clarksville shall fall into the hands of the enemy."

Stewart College lost a loyal friend and benefactor and an able trustee at Donelson when Lieutenant Colonel Alfred Robb fell in the thick of battle there. And at the Second Battle of Manassas, Colonel W. A. Forbes was killed. It is no wonder, therefore, that the discouraged Dr. McMullen tendered his resignation as President of Stewart College in September, 1862. The Trustees, however, declined unanimously to accept his resignation, and in October met again to receive the following report from their President:

Clarksville, Tenn., Oct. 13th, 1862

REPORT OF REV. R. B. McMULLEN, PREST. TO SYNOD

To the Trustees of Stewart College.

Gentlemen:

By an agreement entered into with you on the 5th day of Sept., 1861, I was to take the College for one year on my own responsibility: That is, I was to engage and pay all necessary teachers, have all the income from tuition, bonds, subscriptions, buildings, etc. In accordance with this arrangement, I entered upon the duties of instruction on the first Monday in Sept. ['61] assisted by Mr. A. C. Hirsh, the former tutor of the College at his former salary. The number of pupils in attendance during the first session was thirty-six (36) nearly all of whom were in the Preparatory department, every student of the former College being in the army who was able to bear arms excepting two from Ky.

On the 20th day of Jany., 1862, I commenced the second session of the Collegiate year, with as favorable prospects as the preceding tho' much troubled in both as will appear hereafter. This session we taught in the Lecture room of the Presbyterian Church which had been kindly offered to us, the College building being occupied by the Confederate Soldiers as a Hospital. At the end of four weeks our brave and dauntless soldiers were overwhelmed at Fort Donelson thereby causing the surrender of both place and men into the hands of the enemy. At the end of another week the Federals came to this city and the parents thinking it unsafe for their children to pass through the streets on account of the enemies soldiery, the school was closed on the 21st of February. The latter part of March I attempted to revive it but for the reason above stated, the effort was without success and, being attacked with erysipelas, I abandoned all hope of resuscitating the school during the Summer.

The Boarding house of the College was taken by the Confederate Army. The 7th of Jan., '62, brought the demand for the entire College for Hospital purposes, which demand was of course at once cheerfully complied with. And this was followed on the 22nd of Jan. by an order from Col. Wm. A. Quarles, the Commandant of this post, that the Prest. should immediately vacate his residence in the College building for additional Hospital accommodations. This order was likewise complied with the following day and I moved to the house of Prof. Forbes.

Upon the arrival of the Federal soldiers here the Confederate sick and wounded were moved from the College and that building was used by the Federals for a similar purpose. The conduct of these last while occupying the College building was characterized by the grossest vandalism. Notwithstanding their solemn and oft repeated promises to respect and protect the property, they themselves, yes, the very officers who made these promises, four several times forced the doors of the cabinet rooms, broke open the cases of mineralogical and geological specimens and carried away many of the most valuable specimens, and choice portion of the books belonging to the Washington Irving Society, chairs, tables, curtains, etc., finally stripping even the College chapel of everything in it. The soldiers thus acting were in the building only about a month. They left on the 25th of March taking everything from the College, my cooking stove and other property, besides having seriously damaged the building and utterly destroyed all the furniture. Immediately upon their departure I placed a family in the building with a view of protecting it, but about the middle of April other soldiers took possession of it. The chief officers occupied my residence for their quarters and used my *parlor* for their *kitchen.*

These were quite as lavish in good promises as their predecessors and equally reckless in regard to fulfilling them. In respect to the former vandalism I addressed a note to Col. Bayne of whom I certainly had hoped better things stating the excesses and oppressions of his inferiors in office. On the morning of the 25th of March his men being in the door ready to start to the boat, he sent for me and handed me a reply in which he took no notice of my protest, except to berate me soundly for asking such a thing, while I was not loyal to the United States. It may not perhaps be amiss for me to put on record that those who came in April and continued until the 18th of August were the 71st Reg. Ohio Vol. who were disgraced at Pittsburg Landing or Shiloh for running from their enemies as fast and as far as practicable and who so disgracefully surrendered here, to a very small force without firing a gun.

From the varied facts disclosed above, the pecuniary receipts of the College were very small. That from the pupils being necessarily but little and much of the endowment funds being uncollected, and the Boarding house from which I had hoped to realize something being entirely lost to me. Now this is in many respects a dark picture but I have the utmost confidence both in regard to the College and Country, that the darkness will soon be dissipated, and the clear, bright light of liberty, honesty and love will soon cover the land.

Being solicited by several of the citizens to commence the exercises of the College again, without waiting till the 1st Monday of September, our usual time, and having agreed with you to take the College another year upon the same terms I did the last year, I recommenced teaching on the 11th of Aug. and soon had 30 pupils, about a third of whom were about 15 years of age, and the others mere lads. On Monday, the 18th day of Aug., Cols. Johnson and Woodward, Confederate Commanders of Cavalry made a dash upon the Federal garrison here and captured them as above stated. This produced a war-fever which attacked all my larger boys and they left their studies and took up guns. I asked no one of them to stay but promptly refunded their money. I continued with the younger boys another month. In the meantime a number of men from Fort Donelson bearing the honored name of soldier, but being in spirit highwaymen came and took possession of Clarksville. Their outrages were so great that some of the parents sent their children into the country. Seeing no hope therefore of continuing the school with profit I closed it entirely on the 12th of Sept. And as I could see no prospect of being able to teach for a considerable time and believing that the interest of the College would be promoted by its discontinuance for a season, and allowing me to go into some other business, I offered my resignation on the 11th of September, which you saw proper to decline receiving, but concluding to allow me in the meantime to engage in such other business as I wished.

On the same day of Sept. at a meeting of your Board it was deemed advisable to appoint competent workmen, or other persons to examine into and report upon the damages to the College by the Army during the last year. In accordance with your request I saw the persons appointed by you, took them to the premises, had the examination made, and reports thereof presented. These damages were done in a small degree by our own Army soldiers, but almost wholly by the Federal Army. They consist in injuries done to the building, grounds, fences, furniture, cabinets, chemicals, apparatus, etc., etc.

The total amount of damages assessed as given to and agreed upon by the Board is $10,780.50 besides the damage arising from having closed the College exercises so long. It is hoped that this amount of damages may yet be obtained in some way through our Government. I still hope through the goodness of God that sometime during the present collegiate year we may be allowed to resume our exercises and be able to prosecute our duties as before.

It is also my painful duty to report through you, and in your behalf to the Synod of Nashville in reference to the decease of Cols. A. Robb and W. A. Forbes. The Board deeply afflicted and in great sorrow report that on the 17th of Feby. Col. A. Robb one of our number was removed from earth by a wound received in battle on the 15th while defending our rights and liberties at Fort Donelson. Col. Robb was one of our most liberal and efficient Trustees and an unwavering friend of the College. We feel that our loss is great in his removal from earth, but are happy in being able to say that we have not a shadow of doubt that the Saviour whom he served has taken him to himself. Nor is this the only affliction we are called upon to bear—On the first day of Sept. Col. Wm. A. Forbes, our Prof. of Mathematics, was called to a world of peace by a wound received the preceding day on the field of battle at Manassas while repelling our ruthless invaders from the sacred soil of his native Virginia. Col. Forbes was an able Professor and a successful instructor in his department and it will be difficult for us to fill his chair with one in every way so well qualified and with a heart so devoted to the interest of the Institution. But the God of Providence, who is also the God of love, has so ordered the removal of these two Christian gentlemen from our Country and from our College and to Him we look for guidance to fill their places.

All of which is respectfully submitted,

(Signed) R. B. McMullen, *Prest.*

The meeting of the Board of Trustees on October 13, 1862, was to be the last meeting held by the Board until January 19, 1865, three months before the surrender at Appomattox and the fall of the Confederacy. The report made by President McMullen was adopted by the Trustees and presented as the report of the Board to the Synod of Nashville; and the report of a special committee of the Board assessing damages to the college in excess of $10,000.00 was approved.

The Synod of Nashville, to which this report was submitted, was no longer a court of the united Presbyterian Church as it had been when Stewart College was established. Civil war, unfortunately, had brought a schism in the Church as well as in the State. Dr. McMullen, and other devout leaders both North and South, had deplored this separation of Presbyterians on political grounds, and could only hope that the breach would be soon healed when the passions aroused by war had been forgotten, and the political issues giving rise to the separation in the Church had been adjusted.

When the General Assembly of the Presbyterian Church had met in Rochester, New York, in May, 1860, there was little or no evidence of sectional discord within the Church. Dr. B. M. Palmer, of New Orleans, was nominated at this meeting by Dr. Gardiner Spring, of New York, for a professorship in the Princeton Seminary, and was elected by the Assembly to this position. When the Assembly met in Philadelphia in May, 1861, shortly after the Fort Sumter incident, there were only sixteen commissioners from the Southern States present; and a severe conflict took place over resolutions presented by the same Dr. Spring who had nominated Dr. Palmer for a chair at Princeton, at the last meeting of the Assembly.

Although the "Spring Resolutions" were adopted by the Assembly, they were bitterly opposed by Dr. Charles Hodge of Princeton and by many other Northern leaders of the Church on the ground that "The General Assembly, in thus deciding a political question, and in making that decision practically a condition of Church membership, has in our judgment violated the constitution of the Church, and usurped the prerogative of its divine Master."

To the Southern leaders of the Church there had seemed at the time but one thing left for Southern Presbyterians to do. Consequently, on December 4, 1861, the Presbyterians within the Confederate States, through their representatives, organized at Augusta, Georgia, the "General Assembly of the Presbyterian Church in the Confederate States of America." The Presbyteries composing the Synod of Nashville were represented at the Augusta Assembly, and became a part of the new Church. Thus, when Dr. McMullen made his report to the Synod of Nashville in 1862, it was to the Synod as a Court of the weaker division of the strong Presbyterian Church under whose auspices Stewart College had been founded.

The meeting of the Board in January, 1865, of those members "who are able in the circumstances of the times to assemble," was for the sole purpose of recording "their sense of bereavement which they individually and as members of the Board, in common with the rest of the community have suffered" in the death of President McMullen. This brilliant and colorful preacher-educator who had been so successful in his efforts to transform the frontier college at Clarksville into the beginnings of a Princeton for the Southwest, had been forced by war to witness the destruction of his handiwork. He had resented bitterly the taking over of his home in the Castle Building by the Federal officers after the fall of Fort Donelson, the looting of prized mineral collections, libraries, and laboratories of the college, and especially the stealing of his kitchen stove and the using of his parlor as a kitchen by the soldiers. Yet this resentment did not keep him from volunteering at once, when the dreaded smallpox broke out in their hospital, to nurse these same soldiers and to sacrifice his own life as a result.

The remnant of the Board of Trustees of Stewart College who met on this bleak January day in 1865 now found themselves without a president, faculty, or student body; without buildings, equipment, or money; and without hopes for victory of the Confederate armies. It is little wonder that they were utterly discouraged, and that they were able to give little thought or attention to the college in the darker days to come.

On the fall of Fort Donelson in 1862 not only was Clarksville occupied by the Federals, but Nashville also was taken by Grant's forces; the Confederate State government was driven out never to return; and Andrew Johnson became military governor of Tennessee. Johnson continued to govern the State with Federal military aid throughout the war. On March 4, 1865, Johnson became Vice-President of the United States and the notorious "Parson" Brownlow, a noisy Unionist agitator, breathing dire threats against all loyal Confederates within the State, was chosen Governor of Tennessee.

The administration of the fiery Brownlow, as might be expected during the dark days of reconstruction, was perhaps the most stormy, the most tempestuous, in the history of Tennessee; and the Trustees of Stewart College could expect neither aid nor sympathy from the war-torn State in re-establishing their ruined college.

It is not surprising, therefore, that the first meeting of the Board after the close of the war was not held until July 23, 1866, and that the only business transacted at this meeting was to appoint a committee composed of D. N. Kennedy and J. E. Broaddus to have the ruined buildings covered and the doors and windows planked up.

The Clarksville *Chronicle,* which had suspended publication on the fall of Fort Donelson in 1862, was re-established in July, 1865, and in its first issue began agitating for the reopening of the college. "We trust no efforts will be spared," said the editor on July 28, "to resuscitate Stewart College and the Female Academy at an early date. Their success contributed much to our prosperity heretofore and doubtless would do so again." And within a few weeks he again wrote: "The College building, for the last few years occupied by the military, is about to be given up to the Trustees. We learn that Rev. Dr. Wardlaw, aided by competent assistants, will open a classical and mathematical school in it. We congratulate the community on the fine opportunity for educating their boys. From Dr. Wardlaw's experience and well-known scholarly acquirements, we are sure that an institution conducted by him will have no superior anywhere."

And again on September 8: "The military authorities have given up Stewart College buildings and grounds to the Trustees of the institution. . . . As the College buildings have been very much injured while in possession of the military, we hope the government will make such repairs on them as will restore them to something like the condition they were in when they passed from the hands of the Trustees."

Finally, we see the impatience of the editor at the seeming lack of progress toward the revival of the college in this statement made on April 6, 1866: "In rambling about the city the other day, we paused to gaze at that once architectural and educational boast of Clarksville, then known as the Masonic College of Clarksville. . . . We admired the wonderful natural beauty of the place and its mar-

JOHN B. SHEARER

Chancellor 1870-79; Professor of Biblical Instruction 1879-88

velous advantage for being made into a quiet, cool and cloistered haunt for the study and meditation of the scholar. If we recollect aright, this institution before the war was under the control of a powerful and wealthy religious sect and under its auspices had begun to attract much support from abroad. Now only a little corner of this vast building is used for educational purposes, and has grown into a flourishing local school, it is true, and presided over by a gentleman whose attainments would grace the professorship of any University, and yet it is a mere local academy after all. To devote an edifice so costly, capacious and beautiful to a mere local school seems incongruous."

At a meeting of the Board of Trustees on September 24, 1867, the following report of William M. Stewart, Chairman of the Board, to the Synod of Nashville was read and approved:

The Trustees of Stewart College to the Brethren of the Synod of Nashville, greeting:

Dear Brethren:

The undersigned Trustees of Stewart College deem it their duty to inform you of the present situation of the College that you may take it into consideration and determine what course had best be pursued in regard to it in the future.

It may perhaps be known to some of the members of Synod that immediately after the fall of Fort Donelson the town of Clarksville was occupied by the Federal Troops. The College Building and Dormitory were immediately taken possession of and used at first as a Hospital, afterwards as a barracks and then given up to runaway negroes who had been invited to leave their homes and come into town before any provision had been made for their accommodation. These people occupied the buildings for a considerable time or until a large number of those unhappy people who were driven from their homes in North Georgia and sent north as "Refugees" by General Sherman, were sent down to Clarksville and our College buildings filled with them. Here those unfortunate people remained until near the close of the war. It is scarcely necessary to say, dear Brethren, that after such treatment nothing remained of our prosperous College when it was returned to the custody of the Trustees but the bare walls and floors. The extensive collection of Natural History, the ample Philosophical and Chemical apparatus, in fact, the efficient equipment of the College had all disappeared. The cedar fencing enclosing the College Campus was taken up and used for fuel; there is scarcely a window in the building which is not more or less injured and in some even the sashes have been removed; in a word, the College stands in her weeds a monument and witness of the vandalism of the present civilization. The first thing the Trustees had to do when coming into possession of the building was to put on a new roof to prevent the further dilapidation of the walls which were considerably injured. They have also had two of the rooms cleaned up and set in order for the accommodation of a school for boys which is now in operation with an attendance of twenty-six students under the care of the Rev. Dr. Boyd, late of the Presbytery of West Virginia, whom the Trustees elected to the position of Head Teacher on the very highest testimonials as to character and ability as a Teacher. Under the existing circumstances of the College as related above, to establish an academy for boys is all the Trustees feel themselves authorized to attempt, and this they do in the face of an efficient rivalry of a school of similar character already established in town. The terms upon which Dr. Boyd has taken charge of the school are that he shall receive all the fees for teaching and have the free use of the College buildings and with all the influence the Trustees can give him to make the school self-supporting.

The Trustees do not now feel after the evils they have suffered from the events of the war, in their private affairs, that they can become responsible for any differences in the revenue of the school to meet its expenses as they did for the College all the years it was under the control of the Synod, except the last, at the outbreak of the war when it had become nearly, or quite self-sustaining. The damages to the College and Dormitory Buildings have been estimated by adepts selected by the Trustees at from five to six thousand dollars and it is believed that it will require fully the same to reinstate the buildings alone to say nothing of the necessary equipment for teaching a College course. When application was made by the Trustees to the Government authorities for compensation for damages, the Officials who were then still at Clarksville made the estimate at four thousand dollars for the injuries done to the buildings alone and furnished the necessary documents as required by law, which were transmitted to Washington City but as yet nothing has been produced but the remote prospect of perhaps getting one-half of the estimate if the other half can be applied to the purpose of interesting the different officials through whose hands the case will have to pass in its final adjustment.

Therewith will be found a statement of condition of the College funds and securities drawn up by the Treas. Mr. Jos. E. Broaddus which it is intended shall form part of this report and to which reference is here made. It may be proper to observe for the information of Synod that the values set forth in this statement whether of real estate or invested funds toward an endowment have been contributed by parties in this community on the condition that the efficient College with a fully appointed faculty and equipment for teaching a high College course should be established and maintained or else in failure thereof these properties and funds should revert to the original donors. With this full and candid statement of the condition of the College, the Trustees feel bound to say that unless there is some assurance that this institution can be sustained they will feel it their duty to transfer the building to some organization that will support and return the endowment funds to the donors.

All of which is respectfully submitted,

(Signed) W. M. STEWART, *Chairman.*

(Signed) W. T. HUME, *Secy.*

In spite of this discouraging report, the Synod at its annual meeting in Nashville voted to "assert its fixed determination" to continue and maintain Stewart College and to open it with a full corps of teachers at as early a date as possible. All churches of the Synod would be solicited for funds. The Rev. H. B. Bonde from the Synod and D. N. Kennedy from the Board of Trustees were appointed a committee to look after the college until sufficient money could be raised to repair the dilapidated buildings and establish the college on a permanent basis. The Board of Trustees during the interim were directed to employ one or more teachers at once for the purpose of establishing a first-class High School; and Messrs. Kennedy and Bonde were instructed to visit the Synod of Memphis at its approaching meeting at Trenton "with a view of inviting the said Synod to join us in our educational interest."

The Board promptly ratified and confirmed the action of Synod, authorized the committee appointed by Synod to visit the Synod of Memphis, and then waited impatiently for the promised contribution from the churches to materialize in order that the work of re-organizing the college might be undertaken. In the meantime, one room of the college building had been sufficiently repaired and the Rev. Samuel Boyd, of West Virginia, secured by the committee to open a "Classical, Mathematical and Mercantile School for Boys," in this room; but for lack of patronage the school was short-lived.

This was in the years 1867-68. President Johnson had been unsuccessful in his attempt to carry out the mild ten percent plan of Reconstruction advocated by President Lincoln; and the Radicals in Congress led by Thaddeus Stevens and Charles Sumner had determined, or so it seemed to many Southern leaders, that the South must be made safe for the Republican party and the exploitation of the "scalawags" and "carpetbaggers" at all costs. At any rate, in accordance with the Radical program, the ex-Confederates were disfranchised and the suffrage was granted to the negroes.

As a result of this policy two secret organizations came into great prominence during Brownlow's administration in Tennessee. For whatever good purpose these societies may have been organized, both undoubtedly committed many illegal and outrageous deeds. One of these, the Union League or Loyal League, was composed of negroes and the lowest class of whites. "Carpetbaggers" and "scalawags" controlled this league and often incited the negroes to crime. The other of these organizations, the well-known Ku Klux Klan, was organized by the ex-Confederates at Pulaski, a small town near Nashville. With its grotesque costumes and midnight visits, it became a terror to the superstitious negroes, who had recently been given the franchise by the Radical government, and often to the "carpetbaggers" as well. Loyal Southern newspapers were filled with the report of indignities committeed by negroes, "carpetbaggers," and "scalawags" against the disfranchised whites. Radical papers were filled with the account of outrages committed upon negroes and Union whites by the "Invisible Order." Civil war seemed still to exist in Tennessee.

It is small wonder, therefore, that in times like these, the efforts of the Trustees of Stewart College to raise even the small sum absolutely necessary for reorganizing the college failed. It was in the summer of 1868 that the directors of the Twelfth School District, in need of a building in which to carry on a primary school, proposed to rent, lease, or buy Stewart College, and asked the Board upon what terms they might have it. The Trustees met for the consideration of this request on August 8, 1868, and adopted the following resolution:

"That it is the sense of this Board that Stewart College cannot be sustained by the present organization. Resolved: That we propose to sell the College and grounds for $14,000.00. One-half cash, balance bearing interest with a lien on property subject to the ratification of the Synod of Nashville, and that we decline to lease it upon any terms."

The President of the Board was then directed to "lay before the Synod of Nashville the condition of Stewart College, to represent the propriety of restoring to the original subscribers the sums which they had invested in the endowment fund and to ask authority to make such disposition of the college grounds and buildings as the Trustees residing at Clarksville or a majority of them may think best to be done."

At its October meeting in 1868, therefore, the Synod was presented with the following report signed by William M. Stewart as Chairman of the Board:

The Board of Trustees of Stewart College and Synod of Nashville: Greeting. Dear Brethren.

Since our last report of the condition of Stewart College very little has been done with it. We have permitted Mr. Quarles, an accomplished teacher, to occupy a part of the College Building for school purposes which he has free of rent: he has collected about sixty boys into his classes and will by agreement continue to occupy these apartments during the present scholastic year. In the meantime the College edifice is in the same state of dilapidation as at our last report except a few repairs which were absolutely necessary to the rooms occupied by Mr. Quarles before he could go into them.

We have to regret that the efforts made to raise funds for the reestablishing of the College as suggested by Synod at its last session are without the desired results. The committee appointed by Synod to go to Memphis at the session of the Synod there, having done so were received with kindness and sympathy but were not encouraged to hope for any immediate assistance, and the circular letter addressed by these gentlemen to the churches has been absolutely without effect or response. The mission of Rev. Dr. Wardlaw who was appointed as agent to represent the claims of the College to the churches and people in our connection was almost equally without a favorable result. Dr. Wardlaw made a short excursion in the direction of Kentucky but met with so little success that he returned quite discouraged and has not since resumed his mission. In the midst of these unhappy financial conditions the Trustees learn that the Masonic bodies from whom they originally received the College property contemplate making a demand for a return of it on the ground that the fundamental condition upon which the property was transferred, to wit, that an efficient and fully equipped College would be organized and maintained, has failed and the title to the same is now forfeited, and now reverts to them.

In a similar manner is the endowment fund regarded by those who contributed to it and it has been proposed that as the College enterprise has failed that in justice to the contributors the money should be returned to them. Indeed it has been intimated to the Board that if they do not take some measures to wind up the affairs of the College and distribute the funds that a bill will be filed in Chancery to compel them to do so. Surrounded by these embarrassing circumstances and thoroughly discouraged the Board held a meeting on the 13th inst. which was very fully attended by resident members and after a thoughtful discussion of the affairs of the College, the following resolution was unanimously adopted:

Resolved that the President of the Board be directed to lay before the Synod of Nashville at the approaching session the condition of

Stewart College to represent the propriety of restoring to the original owners or subscribers the sum which they have invested in the endowment fund and to ask authority to make such disposition of the College grounds and buildings as the Trustees residing at Clarksville or a majority of them may think best to be done.

It will be seen from the foregoing resolution that the Trustees desire to finally wind up and dispose of the College building enterprise and as there are parties ready to take it off their hands for public purposes it would seem to be a favorable time to close it up so far as we are concerned and particularly as it is in its present condition only a source of mortification and reproach. As the resolution above only refers to the disposition of the endowment fund it may be well in any action Synod takes in the premises to authorize in like manner the distribution of the purchase money originally contributed by the Trustees for the acquisition of the real estate.

All of which is respectfully submitted.

(Signed) WM. M. STEWART, *Chairman*

(Signed) W. T. HUME, *Secy.*

It is somewhat surprising that Synod, harassed as it was with the solution of the financial and ecclesiastical problems of the day, did not welcome the report of the Trustees and rid themselves of the burdens of a broken and bankrupt college, for the seemingly hopeless political and economic condition of the Southern people bore heavily upon the leaders of the Church to whom they now turned for guidance. Reconstruction in the churches was closely related to the same problem within the State, particularly since the South after Appomattox was overrun with religious as well as political "carpetbaggers." The Presbyterians of the North, it is true, were anxious to reunite with the Southern churches now that slavery no longer existed in the South, but many insisted at this time that the Southerners must repent and "confess as sinful all opinions before held in regard to slavery, nullification, rebellion and slavery, and stigmatize secession as a crime and the withdrawal of the Southern churches as a schism." This the Southern Presbyterians were unwilling to do.

Naturally, the Southern churches wanted to hold their negro members, and were willing to make all sorts of adjustments to accomplish this purpose; but many Northern ecclesiastics were firm in their insistence that the spiritual guidance of the negroes must be taken from the "ignorant and impoverished" whites of the South who were incapable "of doing justice to the people whom they had so long persistently wronged." The chief reason, however, for this policy, it would seem, was that for political reasons it was necessary to remove the negroes from Southern religious control. Every religious as well as political "carpetbagger," and, in fact, every Northern agency in the South, worked for separation; and negro preachers were not slow to see the advantages for themselves in independent churches.

Thus the problems of the negro members, of the future relations of the Northern and Southern Presbyterians, of the disorganized and poverty-stricken congregations throughout the South, and of their empty treasuries, would seem far more pressing for settlement when the Synod of Nashville met in the autumn of 1868 than the problem of Stewart College. Yet so necessary would be the educational institutions of the Church in the days to come that the Synod was unwilling to consider hopeless the prospects of reviving the college; and instructions were given to the Synod's Commission on Stewart College to make a final effort to restore the college.

The success of this effort was "as gratifying to the friends of the college as it was unexpected even by the most sanguine." The Synod's Commission was able to report in April, 1869, the collection of six thousand three hundred and ten dollars. Committees of the Board reported that contracts for the complete repair of the college buildings had been let, that efforts were being made to secure an outstanding faculty and president, and that plans were being made for reopening the college in September.

The Clarksville *Chronicle* reported on May 15, 1869:

"It will gratify the whole community to be informed that the repairs of the building of Stewart College are in actual progress and under the energetic supervision of Mr. Tapscott, to whom this care has been committed. . . . The Board of Trustees at a late meeting resolved to reopen the College in September next with a President and two Professors, together with a Preparatory Department. The Board is to re-assemble early in June for election of faculty and perfecting of arrangements for the re-opening. Thus this difficult and doubtful question, we may hope, is happily settled. In a few months the College will again be in operation with fair prospects of success and usefulness."

And on June 19:

"The renovation of Stewart College and surroundings is progressing rapidly. . . . The main building is to be newly painted and otherwise improved, and will soon present the handsome look of yore. May its halls soon be crowded with the young men of the country."

And on July 15, 1869, the following advertisement appeared in the *Tobacco-Leaf:*

STEWART COLLEGE, CLARKSVILLE, TENNESSEE

Rev. Jas. A. Lyon, D.D.—President-elect and Prof. of Ethics, Metaphysics, Logic, Etc.

W. M. Stewart, A.M.—Physical Sciences

Rev. D. Owen Davies, A.M.—Rhetoric and Belles Lettres

Mathematics—(To be supplied at the August meeting of the Board)

Greek and Latin—(The duties of this chair will be discharged by other members of the Faculty until the appointment of a Professor)

Prof. D. M. Quarles, A.M.—Principal Preparatory Dep't. and Prof. of Modern Languages

Expenses per session of twenty weeks:

Tuition, Collegiate $35.00
Tuition, Classical 30.00
Tuition, English Preparatory... 25.00
Tuition, Modern Languages.. 10.00
Contingent Fee 2.00

Board (including room, fire, etc.) per month $15.00 to $20.00
Session begins on the first Monday in September.

IV

Stewart College:
After the War Between the States

ONE OF the most distinguished ministers in the Southern Church during the period following the War Between the States was Dr. James A. Lyon, pastor of the Presbyterian Church at Columbus, Mississippi. Dr. Lyon was keenly interested in the education of the young men of the South, and his great ambition was to see a strong university established by the Presbyterians of the whole South where the youth of the land could have the advantages of a broad Christian education, equal to that of any university in America. His efforts to interest his own Synod of Mississippi in the cause of education, even during the darkest days following Appomattox, were tireless.

To men like Dr. Lyon, interested in the welfare of their Church, not the least of the tragedies resulting from the Civil War had been the breaking up of a united Presbyterian Church into two sectional churches, a division which would probably be more difficult to heal than the temporary division in the national Union caused by the war. These men saw clearly that the hope of the Church now lay chiefly in its educational institutions; for without an educated ministry and without educated lay leaders to work toward the reuniting of the Church and the reconstruction of the State, a divided church and a divided nation would continue to exist for years to come. Dr. Lyon felt, no doubt, that it was the realization of this fact which had impelled General Lee to accept the presidency of Washington College, a small Presbyterian institution at Lexington, Virginia, where he might perform the greatest service for his country.

It was Dr. Lyon who presented to the General Assembly of the Southern Church at its Louisville meeting in 1870 the memorial, adopted by the Synod of Mississippi and addressed to the Assembly, in favor of establishing in the South a strong Presbyterian university, and who made an ardent appeal that the prayer of the memorial be granted by the Assembly.

It was to Dr. Lyon, therefore, that the Trustees of Stewart College turned when in need of a president capable of reorganizing the college on such sound educational and financial lines that it might at once become the outstanding Presbyterian university of the South— the Southern Princeton of which Dr. Lyon and other Presbyterian leaders had long dreamed. It was imagined that he would make the ideal college executive at this critical time, and he was, therefore, elected to the presidency of Stewart College by a unanimous vote at the meeting of the Board on July 6, 1869. Dr. Lyon accepted the position with enthusiasm. The Presbyterians of Columbus and of the Synod of Mississippi, however, were loath to lose their revered pastor and friend. The members of his congregation were tireless in their efforts to hold him in Columbus. The Synod of Mississippi joined in the fight to hold him in their own State. Therefore, with great reluctance, Dr. Lyon finally notified the Trustees that, after all, it would be impossible for him to come to Clarksville and enter on his duties as President of Stewart College.

In this emergency, Professor William M. Stewart, the former President of Stewart College who was now serving as Professor of Natural Sciences without pay, agreed to act as President until a permanent executive could be secured, and the Board wired the Rev. J. B. Shearer of Virginia, asking that he come at once to Clarksville for the purpose of accepting the presidency of the college. Dr. Shearer did not arrive, however, until the session of 1869-70 had been completed under the guidance of Acting President Stewart. Some seventy students had been enrolled during the session, and both the *Chronicle* and the *Tobacco Leaf* were enthusiastic in their support of the reopened college. Said the *Tobacco Leaf:*

"Young men deserving a fine education and thorough training will find no better opportunity offered them than Stewart College affords. Every friend of education should lend a helping hand, even if it be at some sacrifice. With the proper efforts of a united people it will not only soon be self-supporting but will also be a source of great profit by stopping here large sums usually spent farther North for education."

Acting President Stewart, who was also chairman of the Board of Trustees, had been particularly anxious to secure a young man of vision, one thoroughly trained in sound religious, classical, and scientific scholarship of the day, to head the college. In Dr. Shearer he felt that he had found just such a man. At this time the University of Virginia was admittedly the outstanding classical and scientific university of the South, and the Union Seminary at Hampden-Sydney, Virginia, offered the sound theological training which the president of a Presbyterian college would be expected to have. Dr. Shearer was in 1870 a young man of thirty-eight years. He had made a brilliant record at the University of Virginia, where he had earned his Master of Arts degree when only twenty-two years of age. He was also an outstanding graduate of the Union Seminary at Hampden-Sydney, and on graduation from the seminary in 1858 had accepted a call to the Presbyterian Church at Chapel Hill, North Carolina, the seat of the University of North Carolina.

Dr. Shearer's vision was that of a university at Clarksville, in no wise inferior to the University of Virginia in opportunities for sound classical and scientific training, in standards of scholarship, and in the brilliance of its professors, but far superior in that its primary object should be not the training of political leaders for the State but the training of Christian leaders for Church and State. As Thomas Jefferson had looked chiefly to the State for the financing of the University of Virginia, so Dr. Shearer would look to the Church for the support of his institution. Jefferson's idea of the purpose of a university education for political leadership had, it seemed, led him into at least two inconsistencies in establishing the curriculum and choosing professors at the University of Virginia. In the first place, his fear of sectarianism had caused him to reject theology as the "Queen of the Sciences," and to make, therefore, no provision for a "School" or Department of Theology at the University. He had accepted the view of the controversial Dr. Thomas Cooper, whom the Board declined to accept as a professor at the University, that "a professorship of Theology should have no place in our institution." Jefferson's fear of Federalism was the basis of his second inconsistency. Although determined to prevent the teaching of religious sectarianism, he felt it necessary in establishing a School of Law, Politics, and History, to dictate a partisan Democratic-Republican course of instruction and make sure the selection of a staunch member of the party as professor in this department. The "heresy" of Federalism must in this way be excluded. Thus, the cosmopolitan Jefferson had felt no hesitancy in narrowing political science to a party platform.

It seemed to Dr. Shearer, no doubt, that the mistakes made by Jefferson in the organizing of his university were the necessary results of State control but could be avoided by the Church-controlled institution. If the Southern Presbyterian Church could be made to see the great opportunity which it now had of establishing a university based on Jefferson's ideas of (1) the recognition of real university standards of instruction and scholarship, (2) the establishment of distinct "schools" in which great subjects were grouped, (3) the securing of great teachers at any cost, (4) the elective system; and if at the same time the Church would insist that the School of Bible be given a basic place in the organizing of the curriculum, then his vision for the Stewart College of the future might be realized.

Therefore Dr. Shearer, on reaching Clarksville in the summer of 1870, lost no time in beginning the reorganization of the curriculum on the Virginia plan, in enlisting the interest of the Assembly of the Southern Church in a Presbyterian university for the South, and in visiting the neighboring Synods for this purpose. At his first meeting with the Board of Trustees on July 8, 1870, Dr. Shearer succeeded in having the preparatory department dissolved and sub-collegiate courses substituted in order that "all classes shall enjoy direct instruction from the professors in their several departments, it not being desirable to place the pupils in preparation for collegiate classes in charge of tutors or men in subordinate positions." He also proposed his first step in reorganizing the curriculum; and the Board announced that the Chairs of Stewart College would at present consist of Mental and Moral Sciences with their adjuncts Latin, Greek, and Mathematics, and that the English Department and Modern Languages would be distributed among the professors. At this same meeting of the Board the aging Professor Stewart was elected Professor Emeritus of Geology and Mineralogy; J. A. Carriger, graduate of the University of Virginia, was elected Professor of the Greek Languages and Literature; and D. M. Quarles, also a graduate of the University of Virginia, was elected Professor of the Latin Languages and Literature. James Dinwiddie, a distinguished mathematician and Master of Arts of the University of Virginia, had already accepted the Chair of Mathematics; and with President Shearer as Professor of Mental and Moral Philosophy, Logic and Rhetoric, the faculty of Stewart College for the session of 1870-71 was complete.

The *Tobacco Leaf,* commenting on the work of the Board at its meeting on July 8, 1870, said:

"Now it would seem well-nigh impossible that the College thus manned should not achieve success. At any rate, we are glad to entertain a fair conviction that in the vocabulary of the future as connected with Stewart College there will be found no such word as fail. By a singular coincidence, the members of the Faculty are all alumni of the University of Virginia. Two of these are graduates and two fairly won the degree of Master of Arts.

"President Shearer—*primus inter pares*—wearing all the honors of his Alma Mater comes to us with high reputation for thorough scholarship and executive ability. To use one of his own favorite words, he comes with a 'prestige,' that right to make his name a tower of strength—*Collegii decus et columen.*

"Professor Dinwiddie—*nomen praeclarum et venerabile*—is an accomplished Virginia gentleman, also wearing the full honors of the great University. His attainments as a scholar, his aptness as a teacher, and his devotion to his chosen profession are of the first order.

"Professor Carriger, a native of Tennessee, is a graduate of the University [Virginia], and in his department stands eminent. The justly celebrated Dr. Gildersleeve said to the Trustees respecting the appointment of Mr. Carriger, 'You can not do better.'

"Professor Quarles, also a graduate of the University, has been with us for several years and is well known to our people.

"We shall hail the advent of these gentlemen as in every way a desirable addition to our community. We shall be much disappointed if the first of next September, when the College opens, be not the beginning of a great and growing success to an institution in which our whole people should feel a deep interest, and which may be made to contribute so much to the best prosperity of our community. Let us do our part and success is assured."

In his first catalogue Dr. Shearer announced:

"We design to introduce as soon as practicable, a Biblical course commencing with the Freshman class, and running through the College course. This will embrace Old and New Testament History, Archeology, Types, Laws, Fulfilled Prophecies, the Unity of the Scriptures, and the Internal Evidences of Christianity. We propose to make this course co-ordinate in dignity and importance with Languages and Sciences, believing that an accurate knowledge of the Scriptures is essential to true scholarship. . . . The great question is: How shall we sanctify a secular education: Church institutions have hitherto failed to solve it, relying on the overshadowing influence of a mere denominationalism. Give us time and we propose to lay the foundations of an intelligent faith in the God of nature and revelation as one and the same God. There is no need that the tendencies of scholastic studies be rationalistic, nor that the tendencies of science be atheistic or even un-Christian. But science and revelation should be woven into the same web. The foundations of faith should be laid every day in the class-room, and the

B. M. PALMER

"The Father of Southwestern"
Member of Board of Directors, 1875-1901

entire harmony and unity of all truth should be the first and last lesson in every Christian school. The work is new and the field. almost untried in practice. We submit confidently that this is the only field worthy of the united labors and sacrifices of those who love Bible truth."

The formal inauguration of Dr. Shearer as President of Stewart College took place as a part of the commencement exercises in June, 1871. The ceremonies were solemn and impressive. The Reverend D. O. Davies, on behalf of the Synod of Nashville and the Board of Trustees, delivered the keys of the college, with appropriate remarks. Dr. Shearer then gave his inaugural address, which was filled with sound practical views in regard to the difficult work lying ahead of the college and its managers.

"His remarks on the duty of those having charge of education in the Southwest to elevate the standards of learning, and to insist on thorough scholarship as essential to the well-being of society were full of truth. There is no danger that the corps of thorough scholars will become unduly large in any community; the only danger is that we may forget all scholarship in our race after the purely practical. We were impressed by his remarks on the value of mental philosophy as underlying all of human knowledge, and all of practical life, as the basis of practical statesmanship, and of all political principles, and of every great social movement."

Before closing his address, President Shearer pledged himself to raise the standard of learning and to devote his best energies and his most earnest efforts to the building up of a college that would be an honor and a blessing to the people of the Southwest.

One hundred and one students, representing the States of Alabama, Arkansas, Kentucky, Louisiana, Mississippi, Tennessee, and Texas, were enrolled in the college during Dr. Shearer's first year as President. The fiery Parson Brownlow was still Governor of Tennessee and the radical carpetbag-negro governments established throughout the Southern States during President Grant's administration ruled with a reckless and heavy hand. The destitution of the former leaders of the great Cotton Kingdom appeared complete, and any hopes for the future seemed groundless. Their thoughts were turned to the necessities of a bare subsistence rather than to the luxuries of schools and colleges.

It is not surprising, therefore, that the most enthusiastic efforts of Dr. Shearer to interest the General Assembly of the Church in establishing one well-equipped Southern Presbyterian university for the entire South should meet with failure. He did, however, with the assistance of Dr. Lyon, Dr. Palmer, and other great leaders in the Church, succeed in getting the Assembly to call an educational meeting to convene at Huntsville, Alabama, in 1871, "to discuss and, if possible, adopt the plan of establishing one grand University for the whole church South, to be under the care of the Presbyterian people."

Dr. John N. Waddel, then Chancellor of the University of Mississippi, and an ardent supporter of the plan, was made chairman of this convention when it met and the whole subject was thoroughly discussed. The representatives from the Seaboard were frankly uninterested, preferring to devote their meager resources to their own Hampden-Sydney, Davidson, and other Presbyterian colleges within their own borders. The convention, however, did adopt a public address prepared by Dr. Waddel and Dr. Shearer, suggesting that contiguous Synods unite for the purpose of founding a Presbyterian university for the Southwest and thus supply, by co-operation, what no single one could furnish alone. This address was circulated throughout the Southwest, and in his "Memorials of Academic Life" Dr. Waddel says:

"This suggestion was industriously and successfully pressed and elaborated by Rev. Dr. Shearer, then President of Stewart College, at Clarksville, Tenn. A meeting of commissioners from five Synods was held in May, 1873, and a plan was then adopted; and in the autumn of the same year, commissioners were sent from the Synods of Alabama, Arkansas, Memphis, Mississippi and Nashville [and

Texas afterwards joined this association], who adopted a Plan of Union, and all the six Synods agreed upon it; and each one of them appointed two directors to meet in January, 1874, and take charge of the enterprise."

This Plan of Union was largely the work of Dr. B. M. Palmer, admittedly the wisest and most forward-looking leader in the Southern Church, and the man in whose judgment all the uniting Synods had the utmost confidence. No one was more anxious than he to see the proposed Presbyterian university tied securely to the Church, but he was wise enough to understand that too intimate and direct a control of any church institution by the church courts would defeat the purpose for which it was established by the Church itself. Dr. Palmer insisted that he had seen too many church institutions wrecked on the floor of church courts by a too intimate control of the affairs of the institution. He, therefore, laid down the principle that the best interests of both Synods and college could be realized by having the Synods elect the Directors and by having these Directors, rather than the college as such, make to the Synods whatever reports would be found necessary and proper in the circumstances. He pointed out that if the Synod did not have confidence in the men thus elected, it did not have to approve their actions, and could readily change the matter by electing other Directors in whom it did have confidence, on the expiration of the term of the individual or individuals in question. Dr. Palmer felt sure that no church court should attempt to try to manage an institution directly, but only through the trusted men of character and ability whom it elects; and, therefore, he embodied in the Plan of Union the important provision that "the sole government of the institution shall be in the hands of a directory, consisting of two members from each Synod, one elected each year after the first, of whom one-half shall constitute a quorum." In the Charter of Southwestern at Memphis this sound principle was later incorporated in the following words: "That the administration of the affairs of this institution shall be supremely and solely in the hands of its said Board of Directors."

These directors met at Memphis on the thirteenth of January, 1874, and for two days heard the addresses of representatives of different cities throughout the Southwest in competition for the location of the new university. The Reverend Robert L. Brock from the Synod of Kentucky expressed the hope that the attention of the Board might be turned to the Central University of Kentucky. General White of Huntsville, Alabama, urged the claims of that city as the best possible location. John L. H. Tomlin presented the claims of Jackson, Tennessee, and Dr. Shearer was heard in reference to the proposal of the Synod of Nashville and the Trustees of Stewart College that the institution be located at Clarksville with Stewart College as the basis of the new university. It was decided by the Board to postpone consideration of the location until its next meeting, which was to be held at Memphis in July. During the remaining session of the Board plans were adopted for raising funds necessary for the endowment of the proposed university, and by-laws, chiefly the work of Dr. Shearer and Dr. Palmer, were presented and approved. The Southwestern Presbyterian University was chosen as the name of the institution and its object was defined in these words: "To furnish to the Church and to the World an intellectual training of the highest standard and moral training on a scriptural basis." It was also provided that "the Schools of instruction in the departments of Science, Literature and the Arts, when fully developed shall be in number thirteen, and they shall be known by the titles following, viz:

1st   The School of Ethics and Metaphysics
2nd   The School of Biblical Instruction including Christian Evidences, Hebrew and New Testament Greek
3rd   The School of English Literature, including instruction in Elocution and Composition
4th   The School of Political Economy and History
5th   The School of Modern Languages
6th   The School of Ancient Languages
7th   The School of Pure Mathematics

FACULTY OF 1890-91

8th   The School of Physics and Astronomy
9th   The School of Chemistry
10th   The School of Natural History and Geology
11th   The School of Applied Chemistry
12th   The School of Engineering
13th   The School of Commercial Science"

The provision for adding to the system "the departments of professional education, Theology, Law and Medicine" was made dependent on the growth of the University and its financial ability to provide for such departments.

The keen competition for the location of the university aroused not only the Trustees of Stewart College but also the citizens of Clarksville to a determination to secure at all costs the coveted institution for Clarksville when the Board should meet in May, 1874, for the express purpose of deciding upon the location of the institution. The Clarksville *Chronicle* on March 28 quoted the Nashville *Banner* as saying: "We are informed by a letter that on the 17th inst. the city of Huntsville voted $50,000.00 in subscription to the Southwestern University by a vote of 655 to 13"; and the Jackson *Herald* of March 21 as publishing the account of "a large and enthusiastic meeting held at Jackson, Tennessee, composed of the leading citizens of every phase of religious and political faith. After a number of stirring speeches and earnest resolutions they appointed committees —one to prepare and issue an address to the people, and another to solicit subscriptions in every district of the county and in every ward of the city. They further gave evidence of their earnestness in the matter by taking handsome subscriptions on the spot." Said the editor of the *Chronicle*, "Clarksville must not lose this great prize! . . . *We will have the University!* should be the determination of every one capable of lending a helping hand to the good work." This determination evidently stirred the people of the community, for on May 9 it was reported: "Directors will meet at Memphis for the purpose of locating the University on the 14th inst. Clarksville has done nobly and we feel sure will receive the University."

This assurance proved well-founded, for when the Board met in Memphis on May 14, 1874, Clarksville was chosen as the seat of the University by a vote of 7 to 3 in spite of the fact that strong delegations appeared from Bolivar and Jackson in Tennessee, Opelika and Huntsville in Alabama, and Meridian in Mississippi, to urge the claims of their respective cities for the location of the University. Clarksville had sent its most distinguished leaders; and able speeches were made by Major G. A. Henry, Colonel John F. House, Judge R. W. Humphreys, General W. A. Quarles, and the Reverend J. W. Hoyt on behalf of Clarksville.

After the selection of the site, the Board next proceeded to the election of a Chancellor. The only name proposed for this position was that of Dr. B. M. Palmer of New Orleans, perhaps the most distinguished clergyman of any denomination throughout the South. He was unanimously elected, and requested by the Board to act as financial agent in securing the endowment of the University. The Board then recorded its acceptance of the offer of the Synod of Nashville and the Board of Trustees of Stewart College to transfer its properties and assets to the Southwestern Presbyterian University, and provided for the temporary use of the property by Stewart College until the organization of the University might be completed. At the same time the Board unanimously adopted the following resolution:

"Resolved: In the location of the University at Clarksville we the Directors do heartily appreciate and reciprocate the tribute of the Board of Trustees of Stewart College which they make to the worth and nobility of Prof. Wm. M. Stewart, especially as a friend and patron of sound learning; and we do hereby assure the Trustees of Stewart College that we will not overlook their request to perpetuate his memory and name, in some suitable manner when we come to the organization and development of the institution."

The meeting of the Board was finally adjourned on the eighteenth of May after authority had been given to Dr. Palmer to approach the Synods of Missouri, South Carolina, and Georgia, for the purpose of securing their co-operation in the establishment of a strong Presbyterian university.

There was much excitement and celebration in Clarksville on the return from Memphis of the successful delegation bringing the news that Clarksville had been chosen as the site of the University. "The enthusiasm with which the news of its location here was received," said the editor of the *Chronicle,* "was we trust but an earnest of the hearty and enthusiastic support it will receive from all classes. To Dr. J. B. Shearer of Stewart College this great enterprise owes its conception and to him in a large degree is due the honor of its successful inauguration. He has labored faithfully and well for the consummation of this scheme, and has had many obstacles to overcome, but his zeal and energy have been untiring. He was ably assisted in the noble work by the Honorable D. N. Kennedy, whose aid has proved invaluable; and success crowned their efforts."

At the request of the University Board, Stewart College, with Dr. Shearer as President, would continue in existence "until the proper time might come for the opening of the University." For various reasons, chiefly financial, this change was postponed for several years, and it was not until 1879 that the college was finally reorganized as the Southwestern Presbyterian University with Dr. J. N. Waddel replacing Dr. Shearer as President of the University.

One hundred and twenty-five students had been enrolled during the session of 1873-74. Dr. Shearer had reported the urgent need of a sixth professor to fill the Chair of Natural Sciences. During the session of 1874-75 one hundred and fifty students were enrolled and Dr. Shearer announced the arrival of Dr. J. D. Caldwell, of New Orleans, to fill the Chair of Natural Sciences. "It is needless to say," reported Dr. Shearer, "that the past efficient management of the school and its future prospects as the Southwestern Presbyterian University, under the patronage of six or more Synods, combine to give us a larger impetus and to incite an ever increasing interest in the work which has been in our hands."

V

Southwestern Presbyterian University: 1875-1888

WHEN DR. PALMER was chosen Chancellor of the new university in 1874, the Board, the faculty of Stewart College, the citizens of Clarksville, and all people throughout the Southwest had felt that the success of the enterprise was assured. Dr. Palmer had seemed the one man whose popularity, prestige, and ability could unite the support of the entire South in behalf of the Southwestern Presbyterian University during the darkest period of reconstruction, when the spirit of intense sectionalism seemed greater than ever before. It was a tremendous disappointment, therefore, when the Presbytery of New Orleans refused to sever the pastoral relations between Dr. Palmer and his church, and Dr. Palmer himself was persuaded by his congregation and the whole people of New Orleans that it was his duty to decline the Chancellorship of the University and remain at his post where he was so greatly beloved and where he had served to make himself seemingly indispensable during the difficult days of General Benjamin F. Butler and the carpetbag regime. It was to Dr. Palmer that Jefferson Davis, himself an Episcopalian, had turned when in need of comfort and advice during his later years; and it was Mrs. Jefferson Davis who once said: "I think he was the only man with a great reputation and large following of whom I never heard an evil word."

When Dr. Palmer had written the session of the First Presbyterian Church asking that they request the congregation to join with him in an application to the Presbytery of New Orleans to dissolve the pastoral relations, that he might accept the Chancellorship of the University, the session had replied: "Whatever may be the course you shall take to dissolve the pastoral tie now existing between you and the members of the First Presbyterian Church, session will do nothing to aid you in it, believing as it firmly does that the Master has not called them to such a work."

Dr. Palmer later wrote:

"In reference to the University, I cannot explain matters fully without covering too much paper. A complete union of the South and Southwest in a broad educational movement has been long lying upon my heart. But the proposition that I should head the enterprise was sprung upon me suddenly, and crossed all the notions I had entertained of my life-work. But upon reflection I did not feel that I could blow upon it in its very inception. I, therefore, accepted the position, notwithstanding the first duties were so entirely distasteful. But the announcement blew up all sorts of a storm down here, and the whole city came down upon me, together with the congregation. After refusing to withdraw my letter of resignation the session declined to lay it before the congregation and stubbornly refused to take a single step until they should be compelled by presbyterial citation. The onus of convincing the Presbytery was thus thrown wholly upon me, and placed me in the most direct antagonism to my own people. The case was fully and ably argued before the Presbytery, and their decision you know. Throughout my position was painful in the extreme, for I was obliged again and again to resist the effort to make it out a case of reference; and the Presbytery was obliged to take its own responsibility in the decision. I believe that I succeeded in holding myself honestly to the University and to the position of acceptance, but in doing so, of course strained my own relations to my people to the utmost."

The University Board was loath to accept the decision of Presbytery, so greatly did it need and desire the services of Dr. Palmer. Consequently, at the meeting of the Board on June 3, 1875, over a year since the Chancellorship had been offered to him, the following letter, signed by every member of the Board, was forwarded to Dr. Palmer:

"Rev. and Dear Sir,

"We, the undersigned members of the retiring Board of Trustees of Stewart College, have transferred the College, with all of its endowments, buildings and properties, to the Board of Directors of the Southwestern Presbyterian University, and wishing to do all in our power to secure the success of the University, feel it our duty, as our last official act, to urge your acceptance of the office of the Chancellor of the University tendered to you by its Board of Directors.

"We are convinced from our experience in the management of the College, and from our knowledge of the needs of the University, that nothing would do more to secure the success of the Institution, and to advance the educational interests of the South-West than for you to accept this office.

"We therefore earnestly urge you to consecrate your great talents, your high position in the Church, and your wide influence to this important work.

"We are satisfied that your duty to God, as well as the voice of our whole church, indicate that you ought to undertake the work. With prayer to God that He will guide you aright in the matter,

"We are your Brethren in the Lord."

This appeal was in vain, and the Board, of necessity, turned to Dr. Shearer to act as financial agent in raising the endowment, and secured the services of Dr. William Flinn, stated clerk of the Presbytery of New Orleans, to preside over the college during the absence of the President, and to teach the classes heretofore taught by Dr. Shearer. After a canvass of the Synods of Memphis and Nashville Dr. Shearer reported in May, 1877, "I am mortified at the small amount of work done and the meagerness of the results, but it did seem that the work had fallen on unpropitious times." These were the times following the unprecedented financial panic of 1873, when the New York office of the mighty Jay Cooke and Company had closed its doors, followed by a general business collapse which extended through President Grant's second term (1873-77) and beyond. Commercial failures for the year 1873 alone exceeded five thousand in number with liabilities of more than $228,000,000, and worse times were to follow.

It is small wonder that Dr. Shearer reported at the Board meeting on June 3, 1878, that he had found the condition of the churches and population in Middle and West Tennessee to be "even more unsatisfactory than a year ago," when things had seemed hopeless.

"I am absolutely at a loss to recommend anything to the Board with reference to the continuation of the endowment work. If the financial condition of the country is improved I feel the work must go on no matter what its difficulties may be, but if matters grow worse I am convinced that my canvass must be a failure except in the forming acquaintances and making many more intelligent friends for the college. All things considered, I am constrained to feel the last year has been the most laborious and unsatisfactory year of my life."

Judge John W. Green of Knoxville, who entered the University in 1876, records as the most memorable event during his student days in Clarksville a visit made by Jefferson Davis, ex-President of the Confederacy, to his former private secretary, then living in Clarksville. When President Shearer, of the University, learned that Jefferson Davis was in the city, he suspended classes and gave orders for the students to march in a body across town to Madison Street, where Mr. Davis was visiting, and pay him their respects. J. T. Plunket, the most talented orator among the students, was asked to make an appropriate speech. This was answered by President Davis, who then asked to be introduced to each individual student. In his excitement, Plunket was unable to remember the names of all the students, but he was equal to the occasion. He gave to each boy the first name that occurred to him, knowing that Mr. Davis would never know the difference. The graciousness of Jefferson Davis on this occasion made a lasting impression on the students of the University.

Perhaps the greatest blow which the college had sustained since the last meeting of the Board in June, 1877, was in the death of

Professor William M. Stewart. This had occurred on the 26th of September, 1877, and the Board now recorded the resolution adopted by the faculty at the time of his death:

"Prof. Wm. M. Stewart peacefully breathed his last, at his home on the afternoon of Wednesday, September 26th, 1877, in the 75th year of his age. This sad event occasions to us as an Institution and as a Faculty an irreparable loss. Connected with this College from its inception, more than a quarter of a century ago, recognized as its principal friend and pilot in the fact that upon its passing into the hand of the Synod of Nashville it was called by his name; acting from time to time in the various capacities of Professor, President, Trustee, and Patron, always trusted and true, earnest and faithful, it is fitting and becoming that we should give expression to our testimony as to the character and worth of him whom the whole community laments. Respected, honored, beloved by all, it is not strange that those who were privileged to know him most intimately, should have esteemed him most highly. The purity of his life, the gentleness of his manners, the modesty and childlike simplicity which characterized his intercourse with everyone, the frank and generous bearing which he always displayed in every relation, these were some of the more prominent features which endeared him to all; while the high order of his attainments, the wide scope of his erudition, the acuteness of his intellect, together with the accuracy of his memory, the brilliancy of his conversation, and his evident interest in imparting to others the rich fruits of his large experience and observation, rendered him a coveted companion of those of scientific and literary tastes and pursuits. And above all his natural gifts and his mental endowments, the halo of a Christian faith and hope so beautifully illumined his pathway and shed a luster upon every work and occupation of his long and useful life.

"His interest in the cause of education, and especially in the prosperity of this institution, continued unabated to the time of his death. The munificent donations made by him to this College, in the shape of his magnificent cabinets, library and physical and chem-

ROBERT PRICE
Professor of History, 1882-1912

GEORGE FREDERICK NICOLASSEN
Professor of Greek, 1882-1914

EDWIN BLACKWELL MASSIE
Professor of Mathematics, 1880-96

ALBERT BLEDSOE DINWIDDIE
Professor of Mathematics, 1896-1906

ical apparatus, will remain as lasting memorials of his generosity and of his zeal in the advancement of science.

"Be it therefore resolved, That in the death of our friend and colleague, Prof. Wm. M. Stewart, we mourn the removal from our circle of one who commanded our profoundest respect and admiration, by his lofty virtue, his brilliant attainments, his exalted generosity, and his disinterested and untiring devotion to scientific study and education.

"Resolved, That we will always revere and cherish his memory, will endeavor to emulate his noblest deeds, and to pattern our lives after his; and that we will stimulate the energies and ambition of the students of the College, by pointing them to him as an illustrious example."

Dr. Palmer then offered the following resolution, which was unanimously adopted:

"Resolved further as a memorial of his past connection with this institution and of his recent munificent donations the building just erected be henceforth known by the title of 'The Stewart Cabinet Building,' in which shall be arranged as soon as possible the mineralogical and other collections which he has contributed, also that the chair of Natural Sciences in the University shall be styled in honor of him, 'The Stewart Professorship of Natural Sciences.' "

In spite of the insurmountable difficulties and the utter discouragement experienced in the attempt to raise the $500,000 endowment during the "hard times" following the panic of 1873, enough money had been secured, chiefly in and around Clarksville, to begin in 1877 the construction of a new building on the college campus. It was this unfinished building which the Board determined to dedicate, when completed, to the memory of Professor Stewart and give the name "The Stewart Cabinet Building."

The first ray of hope for better times had come with the result of the Presidential election in 1876. News came on the night of the election that the Democratic candidate, Judge Samuel Tilden, had defeated the Republican, General Rutherford B. Hayes, and there was hilarious rejoicing throughout the Solid South. The *Chronicle* of November 18, 1876, was filled with the account of the "grand jollification" at Clarksville, to celebrate the election of Tilden over Hayes. As early as four o'clock "a crowd of patriotic people began to assemble from all parts of the country." A brass band came from Guthrie, the Glee Club from Stewart College; fireworks of all descriptions were used, bonfires were built; long processions paraded the streets; stirring speeches were made by General Quarles, Judge Tyler, Sam Hyman, J. J. West, and, in fact, by nearly every prominent citizen of the town. The editor of the *Tobacco Leaf,* according to the *Chronicle,* "was too full for utterance." The immense crowd went wild with enthusiasm and "dispersed at a late hour with the firm belief that Tilden would be inaugurated next March." This joy was short-lived, for it was soon learned that Judge Tilden had not been elected as was supposed. Fortunately for the Southern people, General Hayes, the successful candidate, did not sympathize with the radical group within the Republican party responsible for the reconstruction measures. On his accession to office the military forces were withdrawn from the South; the reconstruction governments were ended, and the State governments again came into the hands of the Southern whites. Conditions began slowly to improve, and by the time that the Southwestern Presbyterian University Board met in May, 1879, the members felt justified in proceeding with the permanent organization of the University and the election of a Chancellor and faculty with the expectation of opening the doors of the University in the following September.

At this meeting, Dr. John N. Waddel of Memphis, formerly Chancellor of the University of Mississippi, was unanimously chosen as Chancellor of the Southwestern Presbyterian University. Both of the Clarksville papers were enthusiastic in their praise of this choice. Said the *Tobacco Leaf:*

"From what we can learn the Board has done wisely in its selection of Chancellor. Dr. Waddel is one of the finest educators in the

South, and under his management Southwestern University will not be long in attaining the high position that it should occupy. Dr. Waddel was for a term of years Chancellor of the University of Mississippi, and has been all his life engaged in educational pursuits. His father was also a man eminent for his success as a teacher; such men as Calhoun and others who made national reputations having received instruction from him. . . . The election of Dr. Waddel was a proper tribute to a very able man. . . . He is one of the seven distinguished gentlemen who have been honored with the degree of Doctor of Laws by the University of Georgia during a period of seventy years."

The *Chronicle*, reporting at length on the reorganization of the University, said:

"The new Chancellor is the Rev. J. N. Waddel. He was long known and revered as the Chancellor of the University of Mississippi. . . . When the interference of the carpet-bag dynasty made the place intolerable to a Southern man, he resigned and has since been known as the Secretary of the Board of Education of the [Southern] Presbyterian Church."

The reorganization of the curriculum required little change, for the plan of co-ordinate schools and elective courses had been adopted already as far as practicable by President Shearer for Stewart College when the college was reorganized after the War Between the States. Eight Schools—the School of Biblical Instruction, the School of Philosophy, the School of Ancient Languages, the School of Mathematics, the School of Natural Sciences, the School of Modern Languages, the School of History, English Literature and Rhetoric, and the School of Commercial Sciences—were provided for during the first year of reorganization. The student might elect any one of five courses—the Master's course, the Bachelor's course, the Philosophy course, the Science course, or the Commercial course. The first catalogue of the reorganized University announced:

"Students will be allowed a large liberty of choice of classes and courses . . . limited by the judgment of the faculty and by the exigencies of classification, except, however, that all students in regular classes will be required to study one or more classes of the Bible course proper *each year* until its completion. Each student shall pursue the studies of at least three recitations per day. . . . The students are subjected to searching and comprehensive examinations, both written and oral, twice a year. Advancement in the classes is made to depend on these tests."

The editor of the *Chronicle* was greatly impressed by the change in the attitude of the student body, caused chiefly by the seriousness of the faculty and the rigidity of the examinations.

"A very satisfactory change is observable," he says. "The students now present the unmistakable appearance of young men who have plenty to do and are doing it. The lounging, listless expression hitherto observable is altogether thrown off, and such a thing as a student loafing on the street corners is not to be seen. The motto, as visible on every face as if it were written there, is 'No time for fooling, good morning.' A rapid increase in reputation and numbers cannot fail to result from so happy an improvement in the morale of the University."

The editor was also pleased with the fact that the recreational needs of the students had been provided for, by the erection of an outdoor gymnasium, the forming of a baseball team, and the organization by Professor James Dinwiddie of the student body into a military company "who are regularly drilled by him in infantry tactics every afternoon at five."

But the establishment of a Co-ordinate School of History seemed to the editor the most important change made by the University.

"As our readers know, we have long deplored the absence of history as a study from the higher classes of our schools and colleges and urged the adoption of a high standard of teaching in this department. We were soon gratified to learn that it is the purpose of the Faculty to elevate history to an equality of rank with the other great departments of Ancient Languages, Mathematics, and Physical Sciences—an equality, that is, as regards the time assigned to

GEORGE SUMMEY
Chancellor, 1892-1902

JOHN N. WADDEL
Chancellor, 1879-88

MAJOR G. W. MACRAE
Board of Directors, 1878-1922

JAMES JENNINGS MCCOMB
Endower of the First Chair
at Southwestern

its teaching, the strictness and accuracy required in studying it, and the prominence to be occupied by it in examination for a diploma."

The opening of the reorganized University in September, 1879, was preceded by both "fire and plague," to add to the distress of the people of Clarksville and the Southwest. On the night of April 17, 1878, Clarksville was visited "with a disaster unequaled in magnitude since its first origin." A fire broke out in the rear of Kincannon's store on Franklin Street and destroyed sixty-three buildings and thousands of dollars in machinery and goods. Fifteen acres in the business district of the city were reduced to ashes. Fortunately, no college buildings were burned, but the students of Stewart College were among the hundreds of fire fighters who worked the night through in a futile effort to stop the flames. The City Auditorium, in which the commencement exercises of the college were held, was burned, and work on the new building being constructed on the campus was now rushed to completion in order that the college exercises in the following June might be held in the chapel of the "Stewart Building."

The "plague" made its appearance in the outbreak of the dreaded yellow fever throughout the towns and cities of the Southwest in the summers of 1878 and 1879. Memphis, the home of Chancellor Waddel, was particularly hard hit. On August 22, 1878, the *Tobacco Leaf* reported:

"This terrible scourge still exists in Memphis. It is increasing with an average of eight new cases every day and as many deaths. Grenada, Mississippi, has been the greatest sufferer. Not a single case has thus far recovered. The tale is told in a few words. The mortality is terrible and but few of us are left to be added shortly to the new case list. Your reporter is the only telegraph operator left. Total deaths over eighty and increasing rapidly."

And on September 5:

"It is hard to give our readers anything like an accurate account of the yellow fever, which is gradually enveloping the whole of the

Mississippi Valley. At Memphis it is still unabated. People are dying so rapidly that the living are unable to bury the dead. Coffins in some of the cemeteries are piled in tiers awaiting the grave-diggers. Brownsville, Tennessee, has twenty cases and has had several deaths. . . . A relief committee was organized Monday, September 2, at the First National Bank of Clarksville, whose duty it is to secure subscriptions of money and provisions for yellow fever sufferers in Memphis."

Numbers of students from Louisiana, Mississippi, and West Tennessee were kept from entering college during the session of 1878-79 by the yellow fever plague, but they fully expected to be on hand at the opening of the session in 1879. Their plans were again interrupted for, in the summer of 1879, the scourge reappeared. It was reported on July 25: "The first case of fever in Memphis was announced on July 10th. Since then there have been 172 cases and 54 deaths." Strict quarantine regulations were adopted against Memphis and the other yellow fever infested places.

Much to Dr. Waddel's disgust, a Nashville paper listed his name among the Memphis refugees in Clarksville. The new Chancellor, however, had moved to Clarksville in the early summer, before the outbreak of fever in Memphis, and was now busy arranging for the opening of the University in September. "He cheerfully pledges in advance," it was reported, "the devotion of whatever powers and endowments he may possess and the utilization of his long and varied experience as an educator to this new and difficult enterprize."

Perhaps Dr. Waddel's greatest contribution to the University during his nine eventful years as Chancellor was the outstanding faculty which he succeeded in attracting to head the "Schools" which had been established on the organization of the University, as well as the adding of a new School of Theology in 1884, with Dr. Joseph R. Wilson at its head.

On the resignation of Dr. Dinwiddie at the end of his first session in 1880, Dr. Waddel brought to Southwestern Presbyterian University, to fill his place, one of the distinguished mathematics teachers of the period, Professor Edward B. Massie. Professor Massie was a graduate of the University of Virginia, which he had entered "carrying three wounds received while in the Confederate army." A thorough scholar himself, he was able to make mathematics, one of the severest of all studies, perhaps the most popular in the University during the sixteen years he was in charge of that department. A colleague said of him, "The students all love Massie because Massie loves all the students"; and Thomas W. Gregory, when Attorney General of the United States in the cabinet of Woodrow Wilson, referred to Professor Massie as a great teacher whom he had loved during his student days at the Southwestern Presbyterian University. Professor Massie still lives in the hearts of his old students. Dr. A. M. Trawick, of Wofford College, who was a member of his classes as a student at the Southwestern Presbyterian University, has recently borne testimony to the brilliant mind and lovable character of Professor Massie and to his ability to inspire his students with a zeal for knowledge and wisdom.

In 1882, Professor Charles R. Hemphill resigned as Professor of Ancient Languages to accept a position with the Columbia Theological Seminary. To fill this vacancy, Dr. Waddel brought to Clarksville Dr. George F. Nicolassen of Virginia, a man who was to become in the minds of many Southwestern students during the next thirty years, their standard of the ideal teacher.

Dr. Nicolassen was, first of all, a scholar. When he came to Clarksville in 1882 he had just received the degree of Doctor of Philosophy from the Johns Hopkins University at Baltimore. His thorough training in the Humanities had developed in him an intense interest in the young men who entered his classes in Greek and Latin, and enabled him to inspire these men with a new idea of study and a new philosophy of life. Numbers of alumni throughout the South have testified to the great influence exerted on their lives by Dr. Nicolassen when they were students in his classes at the Southwestern Presbyterian University. Dr. Benjamin Palmer Caldwell of the Brooklyn Polytechnic Institute was a small boy, living on the campus in the home of his father, Professor John W. Caldwell, when Dr. Nicolassen arrived. Recently in recalling old days in Clarksville, Dr. Caldwell wrote:

"How well do I remember some of the faculty. Dr. John N. Waddel, the President; Professors Coffman, Price, Shearer and the newcomer, Nicolassen. . . . I recall with great pleasure the military company organized at the college and captained by Dr. Nicolassen. It was a constant joy to watch the drill from the sidelines. We boys soon learned the manual of arms and drilled with sticks. Dr. Nicolassen was a hero in our eyes, not because he had just come from Johns Hopkins with a Ph.D., not because he drilled the military company, not because he was the youngest member of the faculty, but because he owned a great big, high-wheeled bicycle, nickel-plated all over."

The generous gift of Mr. J. J. McComb made possible the endowment of a chair of History, English Literature, and Rhetoric in 1883, and Dr. Waddel was happy to welcome Dr. Robert Price, of Vicksburg, Mississippi, to fill this new chair. Dr. Price, soon after his graduation from the Princeton Theological Seminary in 1852, had returned to Mississippi as Professor of History and English Literature in Oakland College. During the following years he had established himself as a leader in his native state and was noted for his sound views on questions of State and Church. His ready wit and deep interest in his students soon earned for him an enviable reputation as a professor at Southwestern. His insistence upon high standards and his mature judgment made him an invaluable aid in the administration of the University, and for many years he served as Vice-Chancellor.

The fourth of the quintet of outstanding men added to the faculty during Dr. Waddel's administration was Dr. Joseph R. Wilson, who came in 1884 to head the new School of Theology, which was established as one of the co-ordinate schools in that year. Woodrow Wilson, the famous son of Dr. Joseph Wilson, inherited from his distinguished father many of the traits for which he was noted. Dr. Wilson was a fluent speaker, intensely interested in public affairs, and after coming to Clarksville soon established for himself a position of leadership in the community. He gave prestige to the School of Theology, and his public lectures were outstanding events in the cultural life of the city.

Joseph Wilson was the son of staunch Scotch-Irish Presbyterian parents, themselves born in Ireland and living on the Ohio frontier when their son was born in 1822. He received his academic training at Washington and Jefferson College in Pennsylvania and his theological training at the Western Theological Seminary at Allegheny and at Princeton. Soon after graduation he became Professor of Rhetoric at Washington and Jefferson and later came to Hampden-Sydney College in Virginia as a preacher and teacher of Chemistry and Natural Sciences.

In 1855, not many years before the outbreak of the War Between the States, Dr. Wilson was called to the pastorate of the First Presbyterian Church at Staunton, Virginia, and it was there that his son Woodrow Wilson, twenty-ninth President of the United States, was born in 1856.

In 1858, when Woodrow was only two years of age, Dr. Wilson received a call to the historic old First (Presbyterian) Church at Augusta, Georgia, perhaps the most influential church in the South in the days just preceding and during the Civil War. His talent for rhetoric and his eloquence as an orator enabled him at once to assume leadership in the fight for Southern rights in Church and State affairs. He was sent by the Church as a delegate to the long-remembered Presbyterian Assembly which met at Philadelphia in 1861 and formally expelled slaveowners from church membership. And it was in Dr. Wilson's church at Augusta and under his leadership that the Southern leaders met to organize the Southern Presbyterian Church. He himself was elected permanent clerk in the new Assembly, a position which he continued to hold for forty years.

Dr. Wilson was a brilliant as well as a hard-fighting and practical war pastor. On one Sunday morning during the dark days of the war, he entered his pulpit and in place of a sermon announced that since a great battle was being waged at that very moment in Virginia and since the Confederate forces were in dire need of ammunition, the congregation would rise and be dismissed after the singing of the Doxology, in order that the ladies might repair at once to the munitions factory to help with the cartridges.

After the war Dr. Wilson accepted a professorship in the Southern Presbyterian Theological Seminary at Columbia, South Carolina, and in the eyes of all Southerners became one of the "Great Three," consisting of Dr. James H. Thornwell, Dr. Benjamin M. Palmer, and Dr. Wilson, in the leadership of the Church. In 1884 he moved with his family to Clarksville, where his home in the heart of the city soon became a gathering place not only for his students at the University, but for the intellectual leaders of the community. Woodrow at this time was a student at Johns Hopkins, but Joseph, Jr., the younger son, entered Southwestern, taking an active part in all phases of college life. The companionship and love and pride which existed between father and elder son is revealed in the many letters which Dr. Wilson wrote from Clarksville to his son at Baltimore, as well as in those which Woodrow wrote to his father at Clarksville during this period.

To Woodrow Wilson his father was the greatest figure in his whole life. He was always "my incomparable father" and never, so President Wilson said, "did I make an important decision of any kind until after I was forty years old, without first asking my father's advice." An intimate friend of the Wilson family said: "I have never seen filial affection and regard equal to that of Woodrow Wilson for his father. It is hard to say whether genuine admiration for the father's ability or unbounded affection for the man himself was the stronger ingredient in this dominant passion."

The fifth member of the quintet, and in many ways the most important of the appointments made during Dr. Waddel's administration, was Dr. James A. Lyon, who for many long years served as Professor of Natural Sciences at the Southwestern Presbyterian University.

Professor Lyon was the son of Dr. J. A. Lyon, who while serving as pastor of the Presbyterian Church at Columbus, Mississippi, had originated the idea of a strong Presbyterian University for the entire South. Professor Lyon was a boy not yet ten years of age at the outbreak of the Civil War, but in 1869 at the age of seventeen he entered college at Princeton and graduated in 1872 with the second honor in a class of ninety-seven members. He then studied law for two years at the University of Mississippi, receiving the degree of LL.B. in 1874. Later he again entered Princeton, receiving the degree of A.M. from that institution in 1875, and the degree of Ph.D. in 1882.

Before coming to Clarksville, Dr. Lyon served as Professor of Chemistry and Physics in Washington and Jefferson College. He soon established a reputation for thorough and conscientious work, and his department at Southwestern Presbyterian University was kept constantly abreast of the times. His public lectures on scientific subjects were enthusiastically attended by the citizens of Clarksville and the surrounding territory, as well as by the professors and students of the University. His field trips with the students during the session and during the summer vacation were eagerly anticipated by the members of his classes.

Dr. Lyon was an elder in the Presbyterian Church at Clarksville and for many years was superintendent of the Sunday school. He was very fond of all field sports, and did what he could to encourage all desirable forms of athletics among the students. This active interest in their recreational life brought Dr. Lyon into very close touch with the members of the student body, and enabled him to exert a lasting influence on the lives of the young men with whom he came in contact. His home became a popular gathering place for the students, especially after his sons entered the University, for Dr. Lyon was never too tired or too busy to welcome to his home any students who cared to come; and he seemed always ready to discuss with them whatever subjects they themselves might be interested in at the moment.

Dr. Waddel's great ambition was finally realized in the establishment of the School of Theology in 1884. In his inaugural address as Chancellor of the University he had spoken of the objection raised by some to the introduction of religious teaching in a university devoted to the pursuit of literature and science, but he warned that it had better be at once understood that there was to be no uncertainty on that head. The members of the faculty, he said, might be ever so willing to accept suggestions looking to modern improvement in the various departments of education, but on this matter their purpose was fixed and immovable.

"Those who object to education on these principles must go elsewhere for it. There is no need for perpetual inculcation of theological dogma, but the religious needs of the student can be best insured by providing that the teachers employed shall be Christian men, who by the silent influence of their daily life shall inculcate the principles of Christian religion and who on every occasion, for counsel or reproof, for encouragement or reprimand, shall appeal to religious sanctions for the enforcement of their words and acts."

These were the ideas of Dr. Palmer as well, without whose aid the University could never have been established, nor would it have survived. It is true that Dr. Palmer had felt obliged to decline the Chancellorship of the University, but as the most influential member of the Board of Directors during the critical decades of the seventies and eighties, he had been tireless in his efforts to make of the Southwestern Presbyterian University the outstanding example of what a Christian college should be. It was Dr. Palmer whose influence and encouragement made possible the financing of the new School of Theology in 1884, and it was for him the women of New Orleans, who were responsible for completing the endowment of the chair of Theology, asked to name this chair the Palmer Professorship of Theology.

Student life at the University during the eighties and nineties centered in the two literary societies. There was no great stadium and no great "varsity" football team, yet the colorful contests arranged by the Washington Irving and Stewart Societies furnished many college "heroes" and provided to a large extent for the exciting social life of the students. Attractive clubrooms and libraries were fitted up by each society. The young ladies of the community became loyal partisans of one or the other of these societies, and the public debates arranged throughout the term were the outstanding social events of the year. So much time did the students spend on the work of the societies that they solemnly petitioned the Board of Directors to establish each Saturday as a holiday on which they might devote their whole time to the work of their societies.

Many alumni who were trained in the literary societies during the early decades after the establishment of the University have testified not only to the thorough instruction received in the class-rooms during their stay at Clarksville, but also to the valuable experience gained by them in the serious work of the two literary societies. A surprising number of the alumni trained at the South-western Presbyterian University during the seventies and eighties achieved distinction in later life. Among these were Theodore Brantly, Chief Justice of the Supreme Court of Montana; Rufus N. Rhodes, Editor of the Birmingham *News;* the Reverend J. C. Molloy, of Kentucky; the Reverend J. T. Plunket, of Georgia; the Reverend R. A. Webb, Jr., Professor of Theology at Southwestern Presbyterian University, and later at the Presbyterian Theological Seminary of Kentucky; the Reverend T. V. Moore, pastor of the First Presbyterian Church of Helena, Montana; Judge W. M. Cox of the Mississippi Supreme Court; Mayor E. M. Hicks, of San Antonio, Texas; Judge John W. Green, of Knoxville, Tennessee; Dr. James R. Howerton, Professor of Philosophy at Washington and Lee University; Dr. E. W. Fay, Professor at the University of Texas; Judge Thomas Jennings Bailey, Associate Justice of the Supreme Court of the District of Columbia; Thomas Watt Gregory, Attorney General of the United States in President Wilson's Cabinet; Preston C. West, Assistant Attorney General of the United States in 1913; William C. Fitts, Assistant Attorney General of the United States during World War I; Senator Key Pittman of Nevada; Congressman Hugh S. Hersman of California; James Culberson, federal attorney, of Durant, Oklahoma; Judge William L. Frierson, Solicitor General of the United States; Professor John H.

Boyd, of McCormick Theological Seminary; Dr. Theron H. Rice, Professor of English Bible at Union Theological Seminary in Virginia; Dr. A. F. Carr, pastor of the First Presbyterian Church of Savannah, Georgia; Dr. John M. Wells, President of Columbia Theological Seminary; President Samuel E. Chandler of Daniel Baker College, Texas; the Reverend R. A. Haden, missionary to China; the Reverend James F. Johnson, missionary to China; the Reverend Frank A. Cowan, missionary to Brazil; Henry B. Price, missionary to Japan; the Reverend Fred R. Graves of Mississippi; Professor Daniel J. Brimm of the Presbyterian College of South Carolina; the Reverend R. E. McAlpine, missionary to Japan; President Eugene R. Long of Arkansas College; Dr. John M. Mecklin, Professor of Sociology at Dartmouth College; Dr. E. C. Ellett of Memphis; and President John King Ottley of the Fourth National Bank of Atlanta.

Many other prominent alumni of this period might be mentioned, for it was said that the University furnished one-fifth of the ministers of the Southern Presbyterian Church and more than one-third of the ministers of that Church in the Southwestern section which the University primarily served.

In May, 1885, R. F. Craig, representing the Washington Irving Society of Southwestern Presbyterian University, won the orator's medal at the State intercollegiate contest held in Nashville. The *Chronicle* reported:

"On his return to this city he was met at the depot by his fellow students in full force who had employed a brass band for the occasion. They brought him up town in an open hack decorated with flags and drawn by Gill's spanking team of grays. A reception was held at the Court House where M. Savage, Esq., was called on to preside. Speeches of welcome were made by W. C. Fitts and W. M. Anderson representing respectively the Stewart and the Washington Irving Societies. Mr. Craig responded in a short and well-timed speech. Messrs. G. M. Bell, Harry Johnson, Lee Richardson, J. H. Patton, H. Haley, C. P. Colmery, E. M. Hicks, D. Martin and Henry Price made congratulatory speeches.

"We understand that some of the defeated contestants for the medal were much older men than Mr. Craig. A gentleman from California, who represented one of the Vanderbilt societies, was a postgraduate of that institute. Mr. Craig's home is in Crockett County, this state."

A military company, the University Grays, drilled each afternoon at five by Dr. Nicolassen, of the faculty, provided physical training for the students. The prize drills in which members of the company competed for medals and the competitive drills with the Clarksville City Guards furnished colorful entertainment for the community. The *Chronicle* of May 8, 1883, gives the following account of one of these drills:

"The University cadets engaged in a prize drill Friday afternoon the 27th. The object was to ascertain the best drilled man in the company and to award him a handsome gold medal for his championship. . . .

"The company comprises a number of handsome and athletic young gentlemen, and when drawn up in line presents a very prepossessing personnel. The drill took place on the campus, in the rear of the University building. The cadets first formed in front of the University, where they received the Clarksville City Guards, who marched with them to the drill grounds. Quite a crowd, including a number of the Clarksville fair, were out to see the military display. Both companies went through the manual of arms several times and performed a number of evolutions. Each company was very gallant in its demeanor towards the other and the amenities of the occasion were done in good style.

"The officers of the Guards were the judges of the contest for the prize in the company of cadets. After a severe trial in which every member of the company did himself credit, Cadet T. W. Gregory, of West Point, Mississippi, was left standing alone and received the medal as the reward of his proficiency.

"After the contest had been decided, Capt. Rufus N. Rhodes, of the Guards, stepped to the front and presented Capt. G. F. Nicolassen of the Cadets with a very handsome ring. The present came from Capt. Nicolassen's company. Capt. Rhodes had been requested by them to deliver it and he did so with becoming grace in a very neat speech. Capt. Nicolassen seemed to be touched by this token of regard from his men and expressed appreciation in appropriate remarks. When the prizes had been awarded, the companies again marched and counter marched over the campus."

Baseball played some part in the athletic program of the eighties, and we find frequent notices such as the following appearing in the Clarksville papers of that era: "September 6, 1884. A game of baseball was played on the College campus Wednesday afternoon between a club made up of University students and a town club. The students were entirely too much for the home boys. The game was called in the fifth inning and stood 26 to 7."

Even football became popular by the end of the decade, and we find this item among the University notes in the *Tobacco Leaf* of October 1, 1888: "The football made its appearance on the campus last week, at first in the hands of only a few boys but before the afternoon was over about twenty-five enthusiastic fellows were pursuing the ball and good health."

Five national Greek-letter fraternities established chapters on the campus between 1877 and 1887. Pi Kappa Alpha in 1878; Alpha Tau Omega, Sigma Alpha Epsilon, and Kappa Sigma in 1882; and Kappa Alpha in 1887. The chief activity of these groups seems to have been an annual ball and banquet given by each of the fraternities during the college year, to which the social set of Clarksville and neighboring cities were invited. In reporting the social activities incident to commencement in June, 1885, the *Chronicle* states that:

"The commencement season this year has been enlivened by two highly enjoyable social events. The A.T.O. and the K.S. fraternities have engaged in a generous rivalry in their annual balls and banquets and each has striven to surpass the other in the brilliancy and sumptuousness of these entertainments.

"The A.T.O. affair came off in the Tobacco Exchange Friday night, and was in every particular a complete success. The Maltese Cross included in the decorations was 'a thing of beauty.' The banquet was elaborate. Music was furnished by Wehrley's Legion Band of Louisville.

"The Kappa Sigmas were determined to surpass the Alpha Tau Omegas in their ball of Wednesday night. The Exchange building was again brilliant. The Hall was decorated beautifully with the Crescent and Star emblazoned in gas jets at the entrance of the building. The supper table was set in the figure of St. Andrew's Cross, and the banquet was sumptuous. The hours after supper were devoted to the German led by Edgar Morton of New Orleans. The favors were very pretty hand-painted 'sachets.' The Italian Band of Nashville made music for the occasion."

One of the first steps taken by Chancellor Waddel on his arrival at the University was the organization of the wives of the faculty and women of the community into a society for the improvement of the grounds and buildings of the campus. To obtain funds for this purpose a series of lectures, recitals, and concerts was inaugurated by the society, which continued throughout the period an important feature in the social life of the city and the campus. One of these entertainments was a stereopticon art exhibition given in Stewart Hall by Professor William Emery on Monday and Tuesday nights, December 27 and 28, 1870.

"Photographic views brilliantly illuminated by a powerful oxygen-calcium light, representing some of the most interesting places on both shores of the Mediterranean, beginning at Spain with its wonderful Alhambra and Moorish palaces, and continuing through Marseilles, Lyons, Geneva, Florence, Rome, etc., etc. with a trip up the Nile to view the Pyramids were explained by a good lecturer and interspersed with appropriate music."

Drs. Caldwell and Lyon of the Science faculty gave numerous popular lectures on this program, but perhaps the most popular of the entertainers was Dr. Joseph Wilson, Professor of Theology, whose fame was widespread as "an eloquent and captivating speaker." He was always greeted by a crowded house. His audience was particularly impressed by his "superb" lecture on "Courage" given for the benefit of the University gymnasium in October, 1886. "His intermingling of wit and wisdom, jest and judgment, pleasantry and pathos, evinced a master's hand, as well as the most elaborate preparation." The great gift of oratory possessed by Woodrow Wilson would seem to have been inherited to some extent at least from his illustrious father, the Professor of Theology at the University.

Two great disappointments marked the year of 1887 in the history of the University. The one was the serious illness of Dr. Waddel, which made it necessary for him to resign as Chancellor; the other, the withdrawal of the Synod of Texas from the support of the University in order that a Presbyterian college under the control of this Synod might be established within the state. Dr. Palmer especially deplored this action of the Synod of Texas as a return by that Synod to the policy pursued before the Civil War, "of multiplying colleges to such an extent that they all languished through insufficient patronage, with inadequate endowments and with scant and half-starved faculties of instruction everywhere." Oakland College in the Synod of Mississippi and LaGrange College in the Synod of Memphis, both of which had flourished for a short time as colleges under the control of a single Synod before their untimely death for lack of sufficient support, were two examples among many which might have been cited by Dr. Palmer in support of his point of view. He realized fully that the outstanding need of the Southern Presbyterian Church was not a group of struggling colleges, one within the bounds of each Synod, but one strong, well-equipped and well-manned institution depending on the resources of the Presbyterians of all the Synods composing the Southern Church. The withdrawal of the Synod of Texas from the support of the Southwestern Presbyterian University was to Dr. Palmer a blow to the cause of Presbyterianism in the Southwest.

VI ⁊

Southwestern Presbyterian University: 1889-1917

THE RESIGNATION OF DR. WADDEL after nine years of service as Chancellor was a serious blow to the University. To replace Dr. Waddel, the Board elected Dr. C. C. Hersman, of South Carolina, at a special meeting called for that purpose in March, 1888. Dr. Shearer was elected Vice-Chancellor at this same meeting, but soon severed his connections with the University which he had so long and so faithfully served, to accept the presidency of Davidson College in North Carolina.

Dr. Hersman, at the time of his election to the Chancellorship, was Professor of Hebrew Literature and New Testament Exegesis in the Columbia Theological Seminary at Columbia, South Carolina. Columbia was loath to let him go, and Dr. Hersman was reluctant to leave the Seminary. Therefore, when recalled to Columbia after three years at Clarksville, he felt it his duty to return and the Board was again forced to seek a Chancellor for Southwestern. Their choice at this time fell on another South Carolinian, Dr. J. M. Rawlings of Spartanburg, but Dr. Rawlings was barely settled in his new office when he was attacked by an illness so serious that it became necessary for him to resign. Dr. George Summey, then Managing Editor of the *Presbyterian Quarterly Review,* published at Richmond, Virginia, was elected Chancellor. Dr. Summey arrived at Clarksville during the summer of 1892, and continued in office as Chancellor of the University during the next ten years.

Dr. Hersman's short regime was marked by his successful efforts to improve the appearance of the college buildings and grounds. A well-known landscape gardener from Louisville was secured. Walks and drives were laid out; over three hundred trees were planted on the back campus; the Waddel Memorial Building sponsored by the University Young Men's Christian Association was begun; Robb Hall was enlarged and converted into a dormitory for theological students, with funds contributed by the Presbytery of Nashville; and the campus "assumed the appearance of a well-kept park."

Unfortunately, Chancellor Rawlings was not the only loss to the University caused by serious illness during the early nineties. Professor Coffman, who had filled so acceptably the Chair of Modern Languages since the college was reorganized in 1869, handed in his resignation, because of ill health, in June, 1891. Dr. Wilson, who had come to the University when the School of Theology was established, and Dr. Joseph Bardwell, who had succeeded Dr. Shearer in the Chair of Biblical Instruction, for a similar reason handed in their resignations in June, 1892.

The students who returned to Southwestern in September, 1892, found, therefore, a somewhat changed faculty as well as a new Chancellor. Professors Massie, Nicolassen, Price, and Lyon were still there, but Chancellor Summey, Professor T. O. Deaderick, Dr. Thornton Whaling, Dr. W. A. Alexander, and Dr. R. A. Webb were all newcomers.

Professor Deaderick had been Professor of Latin and Greek at the University of Tennessee, but had resigned to do special study abroad in the Universities of Berlin and Leipzig. On his return to America in 1889 he accepted the Chair of Ancient Languages in West Florida Seminary, from which college he came to Clarksville in 1891 to become Professor of Latin and French in the Southwestern Presbyterian University.

Dr. Whaling was brought to Clarksville in 1892 from Birmingham, Alabama (where he was then serving as pastor of the South Highland Presbyterian Church), to become Professor of Philosophy and Practical Theology in the Southwestern Presbyterian University. Dr. Whaling had received his academic training at Davidson College and at Roanoke College, and his theological training at Union Theological Seminary (New York), and at Columbia Theological Seminary.

FOOTBALL TEAM OF 1898

BASKETBALL TEAM OF 1900

Dr. Alexander was a graduate of the University of Mississippi, in which institution he afterward taught Greek and Latin. In 1879 he graduated from the Princeton Theological Seminary. For a number of years he held important pastorates in Mississippi, and in 1902, while serving as pastor of the First Presbyterian Church at Canton, Mississippi, he accepted the Chair of Biblical Languages and Literature in the Southwestern Presbyterian University.

Dr. Webb was the first alumnus of the University to become a member of the faculty. He was a distinguished graduate of the class of 1877. While serving as pastor of the Second Presbyterian Church, Charleston, South Carolina, he was called to the Chair of Theology at the Southwestern Presbyterian University, and returned to Clarksville in 1902, where he would later become Dean of the Theological Department.

Dr. Summey was referred to at this time as "a young man full of what the world calls vim"; and affairs at the University began immediately to reflect the life and energy of the new Chancellor. Work on the Waddel Memorial Hall and gymnasium was rushed to completion and E. M. Mooney was appointed as the first Physical Director in charge of the new gymnasium. Requirements for the degree of Doctor of Philosophy were established, and in 1901 George Summey, Jr., was awarded the first Ph.D. degree granted by the University. A practical course in Engineering was added to the curriculum with a view to establishing a School of Engineering as soon as practicable. Claims against the Federal Government for damages sustained during the Civil War were so vigorously pressed by Chancellor Summey that he was able to secure $25,000 in satisfaction of these claims. The Steers' gift, which had been made years before but which the University had been unable to collect heretofore, was now added to the endowment by Dr. Summey; and with the help of Dr. Palmer, close personal friend of the donor, he secured a gift of $33,500 from Mr. J. J. McComb of New York.

It was during the early years of Chancellor Summey's administration that the alumni enthusiastically undertook to endow the Chair of English, and Professor E. R. Long of Arkansas College at

Batesville was brought to Clarksville as Alumni Professor of English. It was at this time also that Dr. Shearer made a gift of $10,000 on condition that an additional amount be secured sufficient to endow a Chair of Bible. This additional sum was promptly raised by Dr. Summey.

In fact, so successful was the Chancellor in his efforts to procure greatly needed funds for the University that in 1900 the Board decided that it was the proper time to undertake a campaign in connection with the "Centennial Campaign" suggested by the General Assembly of the Southern Presbyterian Church for the purpose of raising one million dollars for the cause of Christian Education. Since Dr. Summey had "shown his eminent fitness for this work," he was asked to devote his whole time to traveling in the interests of the University. Dr. Nicolassen, the Vice-Chancellor, was asked to assume the administrative duties during his absence, and the other members of the faculty were asked to carry on the work of his classes.

Neither the Chancellor nor the Vice-Chancellor had an easy time under this arrangement, and at the June meeting of the Board Dr. Summey handed in his resignation as Chancellor of the University, and the resignation of Dr. Nicolassen as Vice-Chancellor soon followed.

Dr. Summey reported in June, 1902, that "the burden is greater, in some respects, than I can bear, and I cannot continue to undertake it." His efforts to raise the endowment had met with little success. The number of students during his absence had fallen until the total enrollment for the session of 1901-1902 had reached only ninety. The Synod of Mississippi had called upon its directors "to look into the matter."

Perhaps Dr. Summey's greatest disappointment came with his realization that the Presbyterian Church had seemingly lost its former zeal for the welfare of its colleges. Wherever he had gone in his efforts to secure necessary funds for the Presbyterian university of the Southwest he met with comparative indifference on the part of Presbyterians within the bounds of the controlling Synods.

With the tremendous growth of the state-supported colleges during the decade in which Dr. Summey had served as Chancellor of the Southwestern Presbyterian University, the indifference of Presbyterians to their own church colleges had evidently increased.

It was true that since the days of the famous Log College, founded by Presbyterians in the Pennsylvania Colony as early as 1729, and of the college founded at Princeton in 1746, Presbyterians had been famed for their zeal in the field of higher education. It was the Presbyterians who had founded and supported the Log Colleges of the Carolinas in the early days and who had later founded and supported colleges on the Western frontiers before the unfortunate division into a Northern and a Southern Church had occurred. No longer, however, could Dr. Summey and other Presbyterian leaders boast of the pre-eminence of their Church in the field of American education. It would seem that Presbyterians had themselves fallen in line with the steady trend away from the Christian college to the state-supported university, unaware of or indifferent to the special need of the Christian college to emphasize the great moral and religious principles upon which the American republic had been founded. Dr. Summey realized fully the necessity for the religious training of the youth of America, and he sensed, no doubt, the national peril which would surely arise if the Church should turn over the education of its youth to the State while the State should refuse to give the religious training so necessary for the education of good citizens.

Only one month before the resignation of Chancellor Summey the University lost by death the man on whose influence and judgment the Board had depended since the foundation of the Southwestern Presbyterian University. On May 2, 1902, Dr. Benjamin Palmer had been struck down by a streetcar while crossing the streets of New Orleans.

"The sympathy of the Church universal seemed to be aroused, when word came of his hurt, that proved unto death. Prayers were offered in his behalf in the General Conference of the Methodist

Church, in the General Convention of the Baptist Church, in the Conference of the Rabbis of the Jewish Church, in the General Assembly of the Northern Presbyterian Church and in his own beloved Church's General Assembly. . . . Dr. Palmer's love for the University had been second only to that of his love for the Church. From the beginning he had remained the faithful friend of the University, taking the deepest interest in all of its affairs, attending its Directors' meetings, . . . giving of his own means to further its ends, and by work and letter and effort, inducing others to share in the great work."

Since the War Between the States, Dr. Palmer had been one of the few leaders in the Southern Church whose interest and vision were broad enough to encompass the whole Church rather than a Synod or Presbytery alone, and he had been tireless in his efforts to rally the support of the whole Church to the Southwestern Presbyterian University, discouraging at every opportunity sectional division and dissension and the tendency to establish feeble Synodical colleges within the narrow bounds of each Presbytery or Synod. The lack of his broadminded influence and encouragement would be a serious loss to the University in the trying days to come. Dr. Summey said:

"His intense interest in the cause of Christian Education led to his devotion to this University. Linked with the names of Shearer and Kennedy, his name will be remembered as long as this institution stands, for to him and to them does it owe the beginnings of all that it is and that it has done."

In the following year the Board had to mourn the loss of Mr. D. N. Kennedy, the only surviving member of the original Board of the Southwestern Presbyterian University. At their annual meeting in 1904 the members of the Board recorded the fact that:

"The Board in the death of this honored servant of God has lost its oldest, most useful and most honored member, whose place no one can fill. Always bearing on his heart the welfare, progress and development of this institution, he was ever watchful and vigilant to conserve its highest interests. Having served it for more than half a century he was thoroughly acquainted with every phase of its history, and was always ready with wise and prudent counsel and suggestions, freely and gladly giving of his time, means and earnest efforts to advance her interests and welfare."

In spite of the growing indifference of Presbyterians to the financial support of the University during the decade of the nineties, the faculty was able in a surprising manner to continue the sound standards of scholarship established by the founders of the University. This is evidenced by the well-trained leaders sent forth during the administration of Dr. Summey. Dr. Valdemar Moldenhawer, for many years the distinguished pastor of the First Presbyterian Church, New York City, has stated that he himself was so deeply impressed by the scholarship found at the Southwestern Presbyterian University that he could never be thankful enough for what he had received there.

A partial list of the students trained at Clarksville during the decade of the nineties who afterwards rendered conspicuous service in the field of religion would include such well-known names as those of Dr. Moldenhawer; Harris E. Kirk of Baltimore; Dunbar H. Ogden of New Orleans; E. L. Hill of Athens, Georgia; J. J. Hill of Memphis; Robert Hill of Texas; H. M. McLain of Mississippi; W. J. McMillan of Baltimore; J. D. McPhail of Alabama; John W. Orr of Memphis; D. W. Hollingsworth of Alabama; J. W. Mosely of Oklahoma; L. R. Lynn of South Carolina; J. C. Trim of Tampa; George D. Booth of Natchez; C. T. Caldwell of Texas; Walter L. Caldwell of Nashville; R. L. Campbell of Mississippi; C. C. Carson of Bristol; J. Walter Cobb of Tennessee; B. I. Dickey of Texas; Joseph Dunglinson of Alabama; W. B. Gray of Texas; and James E. Green of Arkansas.

A partial list of students sent forth during the nineties who afterwards served the Church in foreign fields would include the names of: W. M. Clark, missionary to Korea; J. S. Crowley, missionary to

Africa; Thomas B. Grafton, missionary to China; J. T. Hall, missionary to Cuba; Alva Hardie, missionary to Brazil; P. H. Hensley, Jr., missionary to Cuba; J. M. McGinnis, missionary to China; and J. S. Nisbet, missionary to Korea.

Among those students of the nineties who afterwards engaged in the work of higher education might be listed the names of: J. P. Montgomery, Professor of Chemistry, University of Alabama; J. A. Lyon, Professor of Physics, Tulane University; Frazer Hood, Professor of Psychology, Davidson College; C. E. Allen, Professor of History, Centre College; George Summey, Jr., Professor of English, North Carolina State College; R. F. Cooper, Vice-President, Belhaven College; W. H. Frazer, President, Queens College; R. F. Fulton, Professor of History, Southwestern Presbyterian University; Spencer McCallie, Headmaster, McCallie School; E. D. McDougall, Dean, Southwestern at Memphis; M. E. Melvin, President, Westminster College; and G. T. Pace, Professor of Natural Sciences, Flora Macdonald College.

A partial list of those students of the nineties who afterwards distinguished themselves in the fields of law, medicine, and business would include the names of: Judge Nathan L. Bachman of the Supreme Court of Tennessee; F. P. Caldwell, State War Historian of Kentucky; W. M. Daniel, Jr., of Clarksville, Tennessee; G. R. Edwards, Treasurer of the State of Mississippi from 1908 to 1912; J. G. Hamilton, President, Bar Association, Mobile, Alabama; G. W. Muir, City and State Attorney, Lexington, Kentucky; R. E. Craig, of New Orleans; Wesley Drane, Chairman of Board, First National Bank of Clarksville, Tennessee; Courtenay Dinwiddie, organizer of the Cincinnati Public Health Federation; Oscar Newton, Director Federal Reserve Bank, Atlanta, Georgia; Dr. Oscar Wilkinson of Washington, D. C.; Dr. W. H. Deaderick of Hot Springs, Arkansas; Dr. R. B. Macon of Clarksville, Tennessee; Editor R. B. Eleazer of the *Missionary Voice;* and Judge John T. Cunningham of Clarksville, Tennessee.

On the resignation of Dr. Summey in 1902, the Vice-Chancellor, Dr. Nicolassen, was asked by the Board to act as Chancellor until

a new Chancellor could be secured. It was at this time that a movement started in the Synods looking toward the removal of the University to a large city where it might more easily attract the support
of the financial leaders of the new South. That this movement
might be stopped before it had well begun, the Board at once took
action at its March meeting in 1903, adopting unanimously the
following resolution:

"Whereas, the members of the Board of Directors of the Southwestern Presbyterian University are profoundly convinced that the
interests of Christian education and of the Presbyterian Church in
the great Mississippi Valley region, which were evidently considered
by the original donors of the funds in our care, would be seriously
jeopardized by the consummation of any such scheme of consolidation as is now being advocated by brethren in Atlanta, and being
further convinced that any such consolidation would, on both moral
and legal grounds, be impossible, we do, therefore, hereby resolve:
That we refuse to consider any proposition, from any source, which
contemplates the removal of the said University from its present
location in the city of Clarksville, Tennessee, or the diversion of its
vested funds, for the purpose of effecting a merging of this institution with any other."

This action of the Board did not, however, put an end to the
movement. Throughout the Synods two strongly opposing groups
developed—the one feeling that the salvation of the struggling University depended on its removal to a large city financially able to
support a great institution; the other, feeling that such a removal
would be a breach of faith with Clarksville and the donors who had
made possible the establishment of the University in that city.

The enthusiastic citizens of Atlanta offered strong inducements
for removal. The Board, however, felt that great injury was being
done to the University by the continued agitation of the question,
and determined at its meeting on April 14, 1904, to appeal to the
"proper courts of the land" to settle the question whether or not

the University could be legally moved to Atlanta or to any other point without the bounds of the State of Tennessee.

Consequently, in December, 1904, the Supreme Court of Tennessee, in the case of *Southwestern Presbyterian University et als* vs. *Presbyterian Synod of Tennessee et als* decreed:

"That neither the Presbyterian Church of the United States, nor any Synod thereof, particularly the Synods mentioned in the pleadings, to-wit:—The Presbyterian Synod of Alabama, the Presbyterian Synod of Louisiana, the Presbyterian Synod of Mississippi, the Presbyterian Synod of Tennessee, nor any officers or moderators or officers thereof, nor the Trustees, nor Directors of the said Southwestern Presbyterian University corporation, nor any other person, company, association or corporation has any right, power or authority, to transfer or remove the said University or College, or any of the assets or property of the said corporation from the State of Tennessee, or to locate the same elsewhere than within the limits of the State of Tennessee, and that the said institution must be maintained at Clarksville, Montgomery County, Tennessee."

At the same meeting of the Board in March, 1903, at which it was resolved to refuse to consider any proposition from any source contemplating the removal of the University from Clarksville, Dr. Robert B. Fulton of the University of Mississippi was elected Chancellor, but declined the position. Dr. Nicolassen, therefore, continued to serve as Acting Chancellor.

A committee from the Board was appointed at this meeting in June, 1903, to confer with the lawyers and doctors of Clarksville relative to the establishment of a Law School and Medical School in connection with the University. As early as 1877 a communication had been received by the Board from Dr. W. J. Armstrong of Memphis in regard to the establishment of a Medical College in Memphis as a part of the Southwestern Presbyterian University at Clarksville, but the Board did not see its way clear to consider the proposition at that time. Sometime later a Law School in Nashville asked to be affiliated with the University, but this proposition was also declined. The committee appointed in June, 1903, found that the Clarksville physicians were in hearty sympathy with the idea of establishing the Medical School and recommended a faculty of thirteen men with Dr. John W. Brandau as Dean and Drs. D. Y. Winston, F. J. Runyon, T. H. Marable, A. L. Macon, R. B. Macon, J. W. Meacham, M. W. Ellis, J. J. Frey, M. L. Hughes, C. H. Cammach, J. L. Slayden, and T. D. Johnson as members of the faculty. The Board authorized this Dean and faculty to organize the School of Medicine, and set aside $1,000 for the purpose of establishing the school.

The committee also found that the lawyers of the city were in hearty sympathy with the proposal to establish a School of Law at the University and that they recommended the Honorable John F. House as Dean and a faculty consisting of Herbert N. Leach, Alex. F. Gholson, and Michael Savage. The Board set aside the sum of $250.00 for the purpose of advertising the School of Law.

Neither the School of Medicine nor the School of Law materialized, however, and we find the Board at its next meeting deciding that "the deficit of $237.27 on incidental, library and diploma fund be paid out of the amount set apart for the Law and Medical Departments a year ago."

Finally, in 1905, through the influence of Major G. W. Macrae, of Memphis, President of the Board of Directors, Dr. Neander M. Woods, then pastor of the Second Presbyterian Church of Louisville, but who had been for many years previous to his call to Louisville the beloved pastor of the Second Presbyterian Church of Memphis, was secured as the new Chancellor of the University.

Preparations were at once begun for impressive inaugural ceremonies to be held in May, 1906, when Dr. Woodrow Wilson of Princeton and Chancellor J. H. Kirkland of Vanderbilt would be invited to make addresses appropriate to the occasion.

Dr. Woods' first great disappointment came with the opening of the new session. There were only some seventy students enrolled during his first session as Chancellor, and he turned his attention at once to the enlargement of the student body. At his first meeting with the Board he asked for permission to solicit funds for the increase of the endowment and betterment of the plant, planning to get in touch with Mr. John D. Rockefeller, Mr. Andrew Carnegie, Miss Helen Gould, and others at once. He suggested that it might be wise to change the name of the University. He secured permission to spend as much as $800, if needful, in advertising the University in magazines and newspapers, "so as to make our school known all over the South." He advocated the immediate improvement of the athletic field, the dormitories, and the quarters assigned to the fraternities for clubrooms. He got the Board to assist the baseball and football teams in purchasing attractive uniforms and in financing trips for intercollegiate games which would advertise the University. He made visits throughout the Synods and received the congratulations of the Board on the cordiality with which he was received.

Dr. Woods soon found, however, that the problems of building up a college were quite different from those of building up a church. He found the Carnegies, Rockefellers, and Goulds much harder to interest than he had supposed. Even the cordiality extended to him by the Synods did not, it seems, imply their willingness to increase financial assistance to the University. In his report to the Board after a strenuous year of visiting various places throughout the Church in the interests of the University, he was forced to say that he was sorry that it seemed necessary for expenditures to exceed the budget made out at the last meeting. He was pleased, however, that "our athletic teams have made such an excellent reputation as Christian gentlemen wherever they have gone" and to report that "our greatest cause for rejoicing was given us by Major G. W. Macrae when he gave us ten thousand dollars."

In spite of the fact that the enrollment for the session of 1907-08 had numbered one hundred twenty, as compared with seventy-four during his first session of 1905-06, Dr. Woods handed in his resignation as Chancellor of the University in February, 1908, to accept a call to the First Presbyterian Church of Montgomery, Alabama.

Dr. Nicolassen had resigned the Vice-Chancellorship in Decem-

ber, 1906, and after his refusal to withdraw his resignation at the
request of the Board, Dr. William Dinwiddie, a newcomer from
Virginia, had been elected to that position. Dr. Dinwiddie had
come to the University as Professor of Mathematics to fill the chair
left vacant by Dr. Albert Dinwiddie, when he resigned to accept a
position with Tulane University in New Orleans.

Dr. William Dinwiddie was now asked to act as Chancellor on
the resignation of Dr. Woods, and in 1908 was duly elected to the
Chancellorship by the Board. One of his first acts was to secure for
the Southwestern Presbyterian University membership in the new
Association of Southern Colleges and Preparatory Schools. He
reorganized the curriculum, providing for pre-engineering, pre-medi-
cal, and pre-law courses. He organized the students into a Boosters
Club, and formed the Student Council for the purpose of encouraging student initiative and student government on the campus. He
urged a new dormitory as the prime need of the University; and
during his five years as Chancellor, contributions to current expenses
and endowment amounted to over $15,000.

Dr. Dinwiddie afterward listed as among the most important of
his achievements as Chancellor, the addition of Professor Scott C.
Lyon to the faculty. Professor Lyon was the youngest son of Dr.
James A. Lyon, who had been for over a quarter of a century the
beloved Professor of Natural Sciences. Professor Lyon had grown
up on the campus, had become one of the outstanding graduates of
the University, and had later done graduate work at Tulane University. The respect in which he was held by the faculty, his interest
in all the students and their affection for him and confidence in his
judgment, won for him the position of Dean. This position he held
until 1925 when he resigned to accept a professorship at Davidson.
During these years his home, just across College Street from the
campus, was a favorite gathering place for the students; and hundreds of alumni, who were students in those days, think of Dr. and
Mrs. "Scotty" Lyon when they go back in memory to their college
days at Southwestern.

Unfortunately, during Dr. Dinwiddie's first year as Chancellor, occurred the death of Dr. William A. Alexander, the revered Dean of the School of Theology, himself a native of Mississippi, and the son of the Rev. J. H. Alexander, one of the most influential members of the Synod of Mississippi in his day. Dr. Alexander "was a wise man." His counsels were sought by the members of the faculty, by the Board of Directors, and in the General Assembly of the Presbyterian Church, of which he had been for many years the Stated Clerk. His death was a serious blow to the University. His place on the faculty was filled by Dr. C. W. Sommerville, pastor of the Crescent Hill Presbyterian Church of Louisville, Kentucky.

Dr. Dinwiddie's policy of visiting the high schools of the neighboring towns; of encouraging athletics and social life on the campus; and of advertising the University in bulletins and through the newspapers was soon rewarded by an increased enrollment. For the first time, the students were able to celebrate great football and baseball victories in addition to the victories of their orators and debaters representing the Washington Irving and Stewart Literary Societies. The members of the football team of 1908, for which two small boys of Clarksville, "Bill" Alexander and "Mike" Savage, served as mascots, won fame for themselves and for Southwestern by tying the score with the University of Kentucky, 6-6, and winning over the University of Mississippi, 9-5, Cumberland University, 23-0, Mississippi A. and M. College at Starkville, 6-5, Union University at Jackson, 8-0, Maryville College, 4-0; and by holding Vanderbilt to the score of 5-11. The baseball team of the same season won over Vanderbilt 5-4, the University of Mississippi, 1-0, Cumberland University 2-1, Mississippi A. and M. 1-0, South Kentucky College 2-1, and Mississippi College 3-2. Needless to say, bonfires and parades were numerous in Clarksville during this session.

By no means the least enthusiastic of the supporters of the teams during these years were "Barney," the Irishman, who regularly appeared on the campus each morning with his basket and cry of "Apples, oranges, bananas, candy, cakes, figs, dates!" and was always present on the athletic field to cheer "his boys" to victory or to mourn over their defeat; and "Old William" and John Henry, the colored janitors, loyal supporters of every team and humble friends of every college boy.

Old William had been born in slavery times, and at the outbreak of the War Between the States had followed his young master into the ranks. After the soldier's death William was persuaded to desert the cause of the South to become a servant of the Northern General Hyman. He followed his general to New York, from where they were sent to Brazil to quell a riot. He returned by way of Mexico, and landed in Galveston, where he was discharged at the close of the war. As he made his way home up the Mississippi, the boat was wrecked and he was one of the few to be saved. He lived several years around Memphis, then came to Clarksville, and in 1886 he became janitor at the University. Many of the alumni of the nineties have said that among the memories of college life which have lingered longest are the memories of "Old William."

John Henry had been first employed by Dr. Summey to ring the old college bell at the end of every class hour. By Dr. Dinwiddie's time he, too, had become a college "notable," and in his later years the students at Memphis affectionately named him "Vice-President" and presented him with a fine watch and chain at the end of his forty years of faithful service to Southwestern.

Dr. Dinwiddie was not a theologian and not a native of the Southwest. He was perhaps more interested in the Schools of Arts and Sciences than in the School of Theology. These may have been reasons why he was unable to win the full confidence and support of the Synods of the Southwest. At any rate, in 1914 he asked the Board to relieve him of the duties of the Chancellor which required so much of his time in the field, agreeing to accept the position of dean, if they so desired. The Board, therefore, met on January 7, 1914, and inaugurated what they called a "Forward Movement" and appointed Dr. William McF. Alexander, representing the Synod of Louisiana, Dr. M. E. Melvin, representing the Synod of Mississippi, and Dr. Sterling Foster, representing the Synod of Alabama, a committee of the Board "to suggest a policy and to find a man to carry it out."

On the recommendation of this committee, the Board abolished the titles of Chancellor and Vice-Chancellor of the University and substituted those of President and Dean. It set aside the sum of $10,000 for the purpose of carrying on a campaign for the raising of funds for the University and the repairing of the buildings of the plant. It then elected Dr. J. B. Hutton, pastor of the First Presbyterian Church, Jackson, Mississippi, as President, and Dr. William Dinwiddie as Dean. Dr. Hutton, it seems, changed his mind after election and his Presbytery refused to release him to accept the presidency, whereupon Dr. J. R. Dobyns of Jackson was elected the new President.

Dr. Dobyns entered on his new duties as President at the beginning of the 1914-15 session. Dr. Dinwiddie declined the deanship, however; and at the end of this session Dr. Nicolassen tendered his resignation as Professor of Greek. Dr. Nicolassen had been with the University for thirty-three years and his loss was a serious one. In 1907 at the end of twenty-five years of faithful service the Board had presented to both Dr. Nicolassen and Dr. Price gold-headed canes as tokens of their appreciation, and they now purchased for Dr. Nicolassen a watch which was presented as a part of the commencement exercises of 1915 with appropriate remarks by Dr. Foster of the Board.

Dr. Dobyns' enthusiasm for reorganizing the University in accordance with his ideas of a "forward movement" did not, it seems, meet with the full approval of his faculty, and he soon asked permission of the Board to reorganize the faculty by nominating to the Board such members as in his judgment should remain and by nominating all members of the faculty thereafter. The members of the Board were not altogether pleased with the success of the President in securing money for the carrying out of the Forward Movement nor with the spending of amounts in excess of the appropriation of the Board for this purpose. At the February meeting of the Executive Committee of the Board, he had reported on a trip made by him to a convention at Charlotte, North Carolina, on which he had taken with him at the expense of the University thirty-nine members of the student body. "We had a special car, decorated with the flaming letters bearing the name 'Southwestern Presbyterian University,' and had with us the University Band, which gave serenades at almost every stop. The papers wrote up the University and complimented it on bringing so many students over the mountains to such a great convention."

Suddenly in October, 1916, shortly after beginning his third session as President of the University, Dr. Dobyns called a special meeting of the Board of Directors, submitted a report on the progress of the University during the two years in which he had been President, made numerous recommendations to the Board, and then handed in his resignation to take effect "within the next ninety days."

One of the recommendations submitted by the President concerned the admission of women students to the University. As far back as 1880 permission had been granted by the Board to daughters of professors to attend "the classes in the institution without, however, reciting in them," and again in 1905 the Board had granted "as a special privilege to the Chancellor's daughter, Miss Alice B. Woods, permission to attend classes at the University, it being, however, understood, that she is not to matriculate but simply to have the privilege of attending the classes as a special favor." The same privilege was later granted to the daughters of Dr. Nicolassen and to the daughters of other members of the faculty. Dr. Dobyns recommended soon after his arrival in Clarksville that in appreciation of the $25,000 subscribed by the citizens of Clarksville for building a sanitary kitchen and dining hall on the University campus, young ladies of Clarksville be admitted; but the Board felt that "The Plan of Union under which we administer our trust gives us no power to make the institution coeducational." At their meeting on October 26, 1916, however, it was decided to admit young women on the same terms as young men in the proportion of ten to one hundred men.

The members of the Synod of Mississippi were greatly concerned over the news of the resignation of Dr. Dobyns. Dr. Dobyns had been one of their number when elected to the presidency of the

University and they had felt that the success of the new policy adopted by the Board prior to his election was assured when Dr. Dobyns had accepted the office of President. The Synod, therefore, immediately appointed a committee of five "to confer with the Directors of Southwestern about the condition of affairs at the University," and invited the Board to meet with this committee as the guests of the Synod at Jackson, Mississippi, on December 19, 1916.

At this meeting held in the lecture room of the First Presbyterian Church at Jackson, the committee at first strongly urged the retention of Dr. Dobyns as President of the University, but after deliberation, decided that such a policy would be unwise if not impossible at this time. They, therefore, agreed with the Board in its action to ask Dr. George Lang, Vice-President of the University, to act as President until a suitable man could be found to assume leadership in carrying out the forward policy already determined upon by the Board.

Dr. Lang was an alumnus of Southwestern, having received his bachelor's degree in 1906. He had been brought back to the University as Professor of History in 1916 from the Presbyterian College at Anniston, Alabama, where he had held the Chair of History. When Dr. Dinwiddie had declined the Vice-Presidency, Dr. Lang, at the suggestion of Dr. Dobyns, had been elected Vice-President by the Board, and his popularity with the students and faculty, as well as his intelligent interest in and love for his alma mater, now made him the logical man to steer the University through the impending crisis, if possible.

Dr. Lang assumed his new position in January, 1917. America entered the First World War in April, only three months later. Immediately over half the student body left to enter or to prepare for entering the war, and the prospects for any students at all during the following session seemed small indeed. Even the optimistic Dr. Lang felt discouraged. He saw the sudden collapse of the revival of college spirit which, with the aid of Professors L. I. MacQueen and I. P. Mason, had been brought about at the beginning of the session. The plans for building two new cottage dormitories, and a greatly

STEWART LITERARY SOCIETY, 1898-99

WASHINGTON IRVING LITERARY SOCIETY, 1898-99

needed dining hall, already under way, had to be cancelled. Not only the students but the younger members of the faculty and staff were within the draft ages. A campaign for funds would now seem useless. Intercollegiate athletics were discontinued, and even the formal commencement exercises were called off in an effort to avoid any unnecessary expenditures.

It is not surprising, therefore, that at the meeting of the Board in May, 1917, Dr. Lang handed in together with his report his own resignation as Professor of History and as Vice-President of the University; and that the Board adopted unanimously the resolution offered by Dr. William McF. Alexander, of Louisiana, that "Because of the present financial condition of Southwestern Presbyterian University, and the impracticability of raising sufficient funds for its necessities during the general unsettlement of the country on account of the war," the Theological School be suspended.

Since its establishment in 1885, with Dr. Joseph R. Wilson at its head, the Theological School had performed a splendid work for the Church. Many of the most eminent ministers in the Church had been prepared for their careers of service in the Theological School at Southwestern. The members of the Board of Directors were, therefore, loath to suspend the School in 1917, even though the outbreak of war had left no students in attendance. For some years, however, it had grown increasingly evident that the Church had more theological seminaries than were perhaps needed, or could be successfully financed, and it now seemed to the Board that the need for a college of liberal arts and sciences sponsored by the Church was far greater than the need for a seminary; hence they felt it their duty to suspend the Theological School in order that they might save the college of liberal arts and sciences. Yet they took this action with a great deal of reluctance and regret, remembering the splendid work it had accomplished in the past.

VII

Southwestern Presbyterian
University: 1917-1925

IN THE DIRE emergency created by the war, the Board turned to
the pastor of the First Presbyterian Church of Clarksville, Dr.
Charles E. Diehl, with little hope that he would be willing to forego
the comparative ease and security of a good pastorate and change
to a new and untried profession in order that he might save and
rebuild their rapidly declining university. To a man, however, they
felt that he was the best fitted, if not the only man they knew, for
undertaking this task. Trained at Johns Hopkins University and
at Princeton University and Seminary, he was a scholar deeply
interested in education. He had proven his ability as a teacher
while conducting the classes in Hebrew at the University after the
death of Dr. Alexander, and had shown unusual executive ability
in his work as pastor of the Presbyterian Churches at Greenville,
Mississippi, and at Clarksville. The members of the faculty had
been impressed by his brilliant and solid thinking as evidenced by
his lectures and sermons to which they had listened with approval.

Dr. Joseph Rennie, Dr. W. McF. Alexander, and Dr. M. E.
Melvin were appointed at the meeting of the Board as a committee
of three "to proceed at once" to the home of Dr. Diehl and notify
him of his election as President of Southwestern Presbyterian University, and to assure him that if he would accept the position he
would have the hearty support of every member of the Board.

Fortunately, Dr. Melvin knew Dr. Diehl well enough to emphasize the difficulties of the position which the Board wished him to
accept. He made no attempt to minimize the seriousness of the crisis
in which the University now found itself, and frankly expressed to
him his own belief that the gigantic task of removal to the city of

Memphis would soon become necessary. Dr. Diehl was equally frank in assuring Dr. Melvin that he felt such a course unthinkable, since the Supreme Court of Tennessee had already handed down an emphatic "no" to the question as to whether or not the Clarksville institution might be moved to Atlanta. The ruggedness of this task which the Board asked him to undertake had an unmistakable appeal to a young man of Dr. Diehl's personality. An easy job would present no challenge. The committee, therefore, was delighted when he agreed to give the matter his careful consideration and let them know his decision at the earliest possible moment.

Dr. Diehl soon agreed to serve as Acting President for six weeks, a period marked by strenuous activity on his part; and then on July 15, 1917, notified the Board of his acceptance of the position as President of the Southwestern Presbyterian University. A vigorous advertising and letter-writing campaign for the purpose of securing students for the fall session, under the direction of Professor Lawrence MacQueen, was carried on throughout the summer. Permission was secured from the Board to remove the regulation limiting the number of young women to be admitted and making them eligible for scholarships upon the same terms as young men. The President was allowed on his own responsibility to try to develop a pre-engineering department and secure a professor for this work. The science laboratories were enlarged and improved under the supervision of Professor Lyon and M. L. MacQueen, who donated their services to the college during the summer months. A bookstore was opened under the auspices of the University and an assistant librarian secured. An athletic coach and drillmaster was employed, and in accordance with the recommendations of the Secretary of War, military drill was made compulsory for all men students of the University. Many necessary repairs and desirable improvements were made on the University buildings, and work on the new Commons, which had been discontinued at the outbreak of war, was resumed and hurried to completion.

It was at this time that Dr. Diehl brought to the University as a notable addition to the faculty, Dr. Charles Louis Townsend, a brillant young Harvard doctor of philosophy, who together with Mrs. Townsend was destined to play an important part in the Southwestern of the transition period.

Only thirty-three of the one hundred and nineteen students enrolled at the outbreak of war were able to return in September, 1917, for the opening of the new session. Forty-one new students made their appearance, making a total enrollment of seventy-four. But only seventeen of the new students, twelve men and five women, were regular students, the remaining twenty-four entering as special students in the night school of mechanical drawing or in special courses in preparation for war activities. In spite of the small enrollment and the uncertainties of the times, the academic standards of the institution were not lowered but raised, and the new President determined to make the college a place where the young men and women whom it accepted as students might receive a sound preparation for life.

As a result of the impressive showing which could be made to the authorities at Washington on the basis of the elevated standards and the improvements in buildings and equipment, Dr. Diehl was able to secure for Southwestern Presbyterian University a unit of the Students' Army Training Corps with Colonel W. N. Hughes as Commanding Officer, Lieutenant George R. Wild as Adjutant, and Lieutenant John R. Brown as Company Commander. This insured a greatly increased student body, and the session of 1918-19 opened with one hundred and eighty-one students, the largest enrollment in the history of the institution at Clarksville.

The adjustments made necessary by the arrival of the military were quickly and efficiently made in spite of the fact that the Colonel was very old and the two lieutenants very young. This year was made memorable throughout the country, however, by the appalling epidemic of influenza which followed the close of the war and the return of the soldiers from the European battlefields. The University did not escape this scourge, which attacked the faculty, the office force, and the student body. More than one hundred and twenty students were ill on the campus, not including many who were sick in their own homes or in the country, and the work of the University was seriously affected. The sudden end of the war, and the equally sudden and unexpected demobilization of the S.A.T.C., presented serious problems not only to Southwestern but to all colleges where these units had existed. Many students left at once for home, and budgets which had been based on the expectation of continued aid from the Government were seriously upset. President Diehl immediately applied for a unit of the Reserve Officers Training Corps, and this application having been granted by the Government, Lt. John C. Bulger was sent at the beginning of the next session to become Commandant of the Southwestern Presbyterian University corps. In the reaction to all things military following the close of the war, the students no longer welcomed compulsory drill, and after one session the faculty agreed to discontinue the R.O.T.C.

Dr. Melvin meanwhile had not changed his opinion that the Southwestern Presbyterian University must move to Memphis in order that it might fulfill the expectations of its founders and the donors of its endowment. On the contrary, this opinion had now become a conviction, and on May 23, 1919, he addressed an urgent appeal to the Board of Directors, offering his own services in an attempt to raise one million dollars "for Southwestern Presbyterian University to be moved to Memphis under the management of the present controlling Synods and the present Board." Dr. Melvin backed this appeal with cogent arguments as to why Memphis was the natural and logical place for the location of the great Presbyterian College of which the Church, the Board, the Alumni, the President, and the Faculty now dreamed.

It was with great reluctance that Dr. Diehl by that time was forced to agree with the conclusion reached by Dr. Melvin; and only his loyalty to the institution which he served could have induced him to consider the removal of the University from Clarksville where he had formed so many friendships. He realized that he would thereby risk the loss of these friends whose loyalty to Clarksville would naturally cause them to refuse to face the facts and admit that an adequate endowment could never be secured unless the institution

were removed to a larger field. Two years of tireless but almost fruit-
less effort on the part of Dr. Diehl to arouse the controlling Synods,
to interest the scattered alumni, and to appeal to the great educational boards of the country had convinced not only the President
but the members of the Board as well, that the very existence of their
university now hung in the balance; and so thorough had been Dr.
Diehl's change of heart and mind since exclaiming to Dr. Melvin,
"This is impossible and unthinkable, since to remove the institution
would be to break faith with the people of Clarksville," that he now
determined to brave the opposition in the city of Clarksville and
accept the consequences.

The Board heartily concurred in the proposition submitted by
Dr. Melvin, and at its meeting on June 2, 1919, appointed Dr.
James I. Vance of Nashville and Dr. William Crowe of Memphis
a committee of two to consult counsel as to all legal questions which
might be involved in removal to Memphis.

In the meantime Dr. Melvin, resting assured that the opinion of
the Honorable C. H. Alexander, expressed in regard to the adverse
decision of the Tennessee Supreme Court on removal to Atlanta,
was sound, did not await the opinion of other lawyers to begin work
in Memphis. Mr. Alexander had said that that decision had not
settled the question of removal but merely the question of owner-
ship and that some day the institution might be removed to some
place in Tennessee if the problem were approached in the right way.

Dr. Melvin and Dr. Diehl soon met with Dr. Crowe in Memphis.
Dr. Crowe "very strongly advised calling into conference one business man of Memphis, who in his judgment held the confidence
of the city, prestige in the Chamber of Commerce, and whose judgment would be invaluable." This man was Mr. E. B. LeMaster.
Mr. LeMaster gave his hearty endorsement to the plan to undertake the raising of one million dollars in the Synods on condition
that Memphis raise $500,000. Mr. LeMaster aided in securing the
endorsement of the Board of Directors of the Chamber of Commerce to the proposition, and both Dr. Melvin and Dr. Diehl felt
that a good start had been made in their progress toward Memphis.

The four controlling Synods met on January 14, 1920, and all heartily approved the plan of the removal of the University to Memphis and the proposal for a million-dollar campaign to be undertaken within the bounds of the four Synods. At a subsequent meeting in the fall of 1920 plans were adopted for carrying out this campaign.

In the meanwhile, at a meeting of the Board on January 20, 1920, Messrs. John Bell Keeble and Currell Vance, well-known attorneys of Nashville, were authorized to prepare a bill seeking to determine the legal steps necessary to transfer the University from Clarksville to Memphis to be filed at the February term of the Chancery Court of Montgomery County, in order that the decision of the Supreme Court of Tennessee might be obtained as speedily as possible. At this meeting the Board also took formal action accepting the proposition of Memphis, made through its Chamber of Commerce, to raise $500,000 on condition that the Board bring to Memphis an additional $1,000,000 and establish a first-class educational institution there.

The early months of the campaign proved sorely disappointing, and Dr. Melvin confessed that "the business situation was so depressed for the first nine months of 1921, that we did very little except spend money." The first city campaign, however, was begun in Nashville under the inspired leadership of Dr. James I. Vance, Vice-Chairman of the Board, toward the end of the year. The goal was $100,000 and the amount subscribed was $103,000. It was the success of this Nashville campaign that put new hope and new life into the whole movement. Then by the Christmas holidays the sum of $200,000 had been subscribed by the citizens of New Orleans in "the biggest city campaign ever put on in the Presbyterian Church, and in many respects the most remarkable." This fund had been subscribed as a memorial to the great Benjamin M. Palmer, "father" of the Southwestern Presbyterian University, and would be used for the construction of Palmer Hall, the Administration Building, the first and largest of the beautiful Gothic buildings to be erected on the campus at Memphis.

Forced to be absent from Clarksville a great part of his time, at work day and night during these strenuous campaign days, President Diehl did not, however, neglect the administrative duties in connection with the University at Clarksville. His inaugural address and his many reports to the Board showed his constant interest in and study of the best educational methods both in this country and abroad. He was in thorough sympathy with the idea upon which the Southwestern Presbyterian University had been founded: that theology was the queen of the sciences, and that a thorough scientific study of the Bible and of the Hebrew-Christian tradition was fundamental in the curriculum of a college of liberal arts. He was proud of the pioneer work which had been done by the Southwestern Presbyterian University in establishing scholarly courses in the English Bible, which were required of every candidate for a degree, and he was determined to strengthen the primacy of the Bible Department in raising the academic standards of the University. He felt that the greatest care must be exercised in securing only the best teachers obtainable, men of the highest Christian principles, trained for their work in the best universities of this country and abroad, and possessing that indefinable quality known as "personality," which would enable them to inspire as well as teach the young men and women entrusted to their care. He was impressed with the tutorial method of instruction used in the great English universities and urged the faculty to introduce this method at least to some extent at Southwestern. A few tutorial courses were established, and the University, along with Harvard and Swarthmore, was among the first in this country to adapt the English tutorial method to its needs, although many other leading American universities have since followed this trend.

In the midst of all the other pressing duties during the summer of 1920, it became necessary for Dr. Diehl to spend much time and thought in filling numerous vacancies in his faculty. Professor C. F. Arrowood, then an instructor at Rice Institute, was secured as Professor of Philosophy. Professor L. I. MacQueen, who had proven himself an almost invaluable aid to the President, resigned during the summer to go to the University of Pittsburgh and later to enter the business world, and Professor W. R. Cooper was secured to replace him in the Chair of History. Professor Cooper was a graduate of Oxford University and thus became the first of that long list of Oxford-trained men who were to become members of the enlarged faculty at Memphis. Professor Warren S. Higgins, a member of the University of Florida faculty, was secured as Professor of Mathematics in place of Instructor M. L. MacQueen, recently granted a leave of absence for advanced study at the University of Wisconsin. Professor G. A. Scott, a member of the faculty of the Georgia School of Technology, replaced Professor Chrisler in the Chair of Physics; and Professor Ralph C. Kenney, then Professor of Political Science at Roanoke College, replaced the greatly beloved "Pete" Richardson, who resigned as Athletic Director to enter the Theological Seminary at Richmond.

The campaign for one million five hundred thousand dollars authorized at a meeting of the Board in January, 1920, had been placed under the direction of the Reverend Henry H. Sweets, D.D., the Executive Secretary of the General Assembly's Executive Committee of Christian Education. On May 31, 1922, Dr. Sweets was able to announce that with the assistance of his field secretaries, Dr. M. E. Melvin and Dr. S. W. McGill, he had been able to bring the campaign to a successful conclusion and that the sum of one million five hundred thousand dollars had been subscribed.

Greatly to the disappointment of President Diehl and the Board of Directors, the decision of the Supreme Court in the University's suit to determine the right of removal to Memphis was delayed until March 8, 1924. But the decision, when it did come, was a clear-cut one in favor of the University, permitting it to remove to Memphis with all of its assets except one gift of approximately $50,000, which was originally made by the city of Clarksville on condition that the college should be located at Clarksville and that at all times there should be ten city scholarships.

The citizens of Memphis were anxious for the removal to take place at once, and for an assurance that the 1925-26 session would open in Memphis. President Diehl lost no time in calling a meeting of the Board on the twenty-fifth of March, 1924, at the Chisca Hotel in Memphis. At this meeting it was decided to apply for an amendment to the charter in which the name of the corporation should be changed from "Southwestern Presbyterian University" to "Southwestern" and the location from Clarksville to Memphis. A Ways and Means Committee was appointed consisting of Mr. W. E. Holt, Chairman, Mr. E. B. LeMaster, Vice-Chairman, Drs. Charles E. Diehl, James I. Vance, A. B. Curry, and Messrs. L. C. Humes, J. D. McDowell, and George G. Tayloe; and this committee was authorized to negotiate a loan of $700,000 to be used in the immediate construction of a Science Building, three dormitories, and a dining hall.

As a result of the first campaign in Memphis, an ideal site for the location of the college had been secured. A wooded area consisting of over one hundred acres facing the city's famed Parkway, and directly across from beautiful Overton Park, in the heart of the growing residential section of Memphis, would be an inspiration to any great architect. Dr. Diehl's realization that he was building for the future, and his conviction that only the best was true economy, had caused him to select Collegiate Gothic as the type of architecture to be used, and stone brought from the quarries at Bald Knob, Arkansas, as the material of which all buildings on the campus should be constructed. He was fortunate in securing the enthusiastic interest and support of Mr. Charles Z. Klauder, well-known architect of Philadelphia, and of Mr. Henry C. Hibbs of Nashville, who furnished him with plans not only for the buildings needed at once, but also for those to be constructed in the distant future, which would make of Southwestern one of the most beautiful campuses in America.

Two hundred thousand dollars had been subscribed for the Palmer Memorial Administration Building by the citizens of New Orleans in the campaign of 1921, and fortunately, work on this building had already begun and was, in fact, well under way when the Board met in Memphis after the Supreme Court's decision in March,

1924. To secure the completion of this building and the construction of the dormitories and science building and dining hall now authorized by the Board, and to have them ready for the opening of college in September, 1925, would be a strenuous undertaking.

Meanwhile, the President and faculty were determined to make the last session of the college at Clarksville the best in the history of the institution, as far as it was in their power to do so. Dr. Diehl had taken care to add to the faculty during these last years at Clarksville, three of the outstanding young alumni of the University, who had further distinguished themselves in the leading graduate schools of the country: Professor M. L. MacQueen, Professor Samuel H. Monk, and Professor William R. Atkinson. These men would be invaluable as a connecting link between the old and the new Southwestern. A second Oxonian, Dr. R. P. Strickler, a former Rhodes Scholar and a Hopkins doctor of philosophy, had been brought from Swarthmore College to fill the Chair of Greek on the resignation of Dr. Clyde Pharr to accept a professorship in Vanderbilt University. Mr. Jess C. Neely, hero of many Vanderbilt football and baseball victories of the early twenties, was now Coach and Athletic Director at Southwestern, and Mr. and Mrs. Woods Harrison, who had come from Nashville to take charge of the boarding department, had already won for themselves an enviable place in the esteem of the student body. Strenuous efforts were made to secure a select body of students who might be able to take with them to Memphis in the following years the high standards and the best traditions of the college at Clarksville.

For the purpose of expressing student opinion on the campus, the *Sou'wester,* a weekly paper edited by the students, had been established in 1919; and for the purpose of giving recognition to exceptional scholarship among the students, Alpha Theta Phi, an honorary fraternity, had been founded in the following year. Student interest in literary attainments was stimulated by the formation of the Stylus Club, which was soon admitted as a chapter of the national literary fraternity, Sigma Upsilon. The Order of the Torch which later became the Southwestern chapter of Omicron Delta

Kappa was also organized at this time. These student organizations would be continued on the removal of the college to Memphis, thus forming an important link between the old and new Southwestern.

Two national sororities established chapters on the campus at Clarksville—Chi Omega in 1922 and Kappa Delta in 1925. The number of women admitted as students at the University had steadily increased since 1921, when in that year Miss Margaret Trahern, of Clarksville, became the first woman graduate in the history of the institution. During the last session at Clarksville there were forty young women among the one hundred and eighty-seven students enrolled—the largest enrollment in the history of the University. Seventy of these students were from Mississippi, fifteen from Alabama, eight from Louisiana, five from Arkansas, three from Oklahoma, eighty-one from Tennessee, and one student each from Illinois, Kentucky, North Carolina, and Texas. These students had been carefully selected and would make a splendid nucleus for the student body on its removal to Memphis.

As might be imagined, the summer of 1925 was a busy one not only for Dr. Diehl but also for every member of the faculty and for many members of the student body as well. The dismantling of the laboratories, libraries, and kitchens, and their packing for safe removal to Memphis, required tireless work on the part of Professors M. L. MacQueen and J. C. Pomeroy, and their corps of student helpers in doing this work. Mrs. Hardy Greenhill, President Diehl's able secretary, was kept busy long after office hours in preparation for the removal. The office of the Dean was flooded with letters, and he was needed both in Clarksville and at Memphis. The two professors having the longest term of service with the University, Dean Lyon and Professor R. C. Beale, had resigned at the close of the session, the former to accept a position on the faculty of Davidson College, and the latter to become Professor of English at Lynchburg College. Professor Cooper was asked to serve as Dean in Dr. Lyon's place, and he remained at Clarksville for the first weeks of the summer, then moved to Memphis, where rooms in the new Robb Hall were made ready for him. Professor Cooper thus became the first resident of the new campus. He found Palmer Hall ready for the opening in September, but the Science Building was far from completion. The crude night watchman's tower occupied the space between Robb Hall and Science Hall, and the old Irish night watchman was welcome company for him when night fell, since there were no homes on the newly constructed University Avenue and only one home on Tutwiler east of McLean. Otherwise his nearest neighbors were the occupants of the zoo in Overton Park, just across the Parkway from the campus.

VIII

Southwestern at Memphis: The First Decade, 1925-1935

THE FOLLOWING EXTRACT from an address delivered by President Diehl, the principles of which were officially adopted by the Board of Directors on February 8, 1922, will reveal the educational ideals and make clear the policy guiding Southwestern on its removal to Memphis:

"While every proper economy will be observed in the planning for and the administration of Southwestern, the fundamental principle upon which all our planning shall proceed is the welfare, and especially the moral welfare, of the students, for whom the institution exists, even though the application of this principle prove to be more costly in dollars and cents.

"Inasmuch as the English system of higher education is in our judgment incomparably better for the moral welfare of the student than the Continental system, we propose as nearly as we can, to follow the English system, with such modifications and adaptations as seem wise.

"We believe that from 150 to 200 students is about the maximum number that should be grouped together as a unit; that such a group is about the ideal size for the helpful development of a common life; and we believe, further, that this number should be broken up into smaller groups for more intimate fellowship.

"We favor, therefore, a dormitory arrangement providing for a unit quadrangle for 175 men, with a common dining room for this group, and a common athletic field and tennis courts.

"We favor also the plan of dividing this quadrangle into five separate groups of halls, each to provide for 34 men and an instructor, and each of these five halls to have a separate living room equipped for each group of 34 students, thus preserving the family idea.

"We are in favor of the policy of having fraternity houses which shall be merely club houses, and not dormitories or residential houses.

"We believe that we can best serve the Church and the Nation by adequately providing for and equipping a comparatively few select men, in accordance with our means, rather than by accepting all who desire to come, and then doing the best we can for them with the limited means at our disposal.

"We, therefore, favor the policy of selecting carefully all students, this selection to be made on the basis of moral character, intellectual fitness and preparation, qualities of leadership, and potentialities of usefulness to church and state, and to limit the number of students accepted by our ability to give them the best advantages, such advantages as they have a right to expect from the standard college of a church which enthrones honesty, and which worships the God of righteousness.

"We believe that there should be, in order to give students the best advantages, an income-producing endowment of not less than $5,000 per student, and it will be our policy to endeavor to measure our student capacity by an income-producing endowment of at least $4,000.00. As our endowment increases and we can provide properly for others, we shall accept more students, all of whom, however, are to be carefully selected.

"We believe, further, that it is for the best interests of the work to have a comparatively small faculty of well-paid professors rather than to have a larger faculty composed mainly of assistant professors and instructors who are serving on a lower salary scale."

Reverence for quality and not quantity, and regard for genuineness and not gaudiness, were the foundation principles on which these ideals were based, and on which Dr. Diehl and the Board desired that the college at Memphis should be built. These were also the principles which had inspired the great Dr. Palmer. Dr. Palmer's vision of a Christian college where, in the words of Woodrow Wilson, "education would be brought to the highest point of development and efficiency, and shot through at every point with Christian principles," was the vision inherited by President Diehl. In order to accomplish this purpose, a School of Bible had been made one of the co-ordinate Schools of the Southwestern Presbyterian University in the days of Dr. Palmer, and at least two years' work in the School of Bible had been required of every candidate for a degree. Dr. Diehl was in thorough accord with Dr. Palmer's idea that the Bible should be made the capstone of the curriculum and was determined that whatever other requirements might be necessary, two years of Bible, one in the freshman year and the other in the senior year, must be completed for a Southwestern degree. He was also determined that these courses in Bible should be taught in the same scholarly method as were courses in Shakespeare, Mathematics, or the Sciences.

This was in the decade of the twenties. The so-called idealism of Woodrow Wilson had been repudiated by the American people. The Harding-Coolidge-Hoover era with its emphasis on the getting of wealth and its love for the spectacular was in full sway, and had wrought tremendous changes in the colleges and universities of America. The popular demand came to be for institutions where the young men of the land might be taught to become successful business men, and the young women might aspire to a successful Hollywood career. The college was apt to be measured, as other institutions of the day, in terms of wealth, size, and glamor. There seemed to be no longer a place, in the minds of the public, for a college of liberal arts and sciences, stressing the fundamental disciplines and preparing its students for the full life, and for wise leadership in Church and State.

The refusal on the part of Dr. Diehl to conform his educational ideals to the trend of the times met with strong opposition. His emphasis on quality rather than quantity was severely criticized. His determination to keep the study of the Bible as the basis of the curriculum was often condemned. His refusal to substitute the more popular vocational studies of the day for Mathematics, the Classics, and History was deemed old-fashioned. His lack of enthusiasm for

CHARLES EDWARD DIEHL

President of Southwestern, 1917-1949

expensive and glamorous football teams at the expense of scholarship could not be understood. Yet no matter how great the criticism, no amount of pressure could cause Dr. Diehl to waver in his determination to build for the future on sound ideals inherited from the past.

September 24, 1925, was a memorable day in the history of Southwestern, for on that date the college opened for its first session in Memphis. The summer had been without rains and the rush to get the buildings ready for the opening day had left no time as yet for the sodding of grass and the laying of walks connecting Palmer Hall with the dormitories, the dining hall, and the Ashner Memorial Gateway. The downpour of rain which turned the yard from a desert of dust into a sea of mud on the opening day did not, however, dampen the spirits of the enthusiastic students who came in surprising numbers to enter the new Southwestern. Two hundred and fifty-nine of the four hundred and six students enrolled during the first session at Memphis came from Tennessee; eighty-seven from Mississippi; twenty-five from Arkansas; thirteen from Louisiana; ten from Alabama; four from Missouri; two from Illinois; two from Texas; and one each from Kentucky, Oklahoma, Pennsylvania, and North Carolina. One hundred and ten of these were women and two hundred and ninety-six were men. Two apartment houses on North Parkway near the campus were secured for the overflow of men from Robb and Calvin Halls, the two dormitories completed on the campus. These temporary dormitories were promptly named Stewart and Waddel Halls, preserving as did Robb and Calvin Halls, names sacred to the University at Clarksville. The out-of-town girls were housed in Clarksville Hall, a large home secured in the neighborhood, and Professor and Mrs. W. R. Atkinson were placed in charge of this dormitory.

With surprising rapidity, the academic and social life of the college got under way. The fine old traditions brought down from Clarksville by the professors and students of the Southwestern Presbyterian University were soon established as traditions of the new college. The same old college bell, which had been rung through the years by Old William and John Henry to summon the Clarksville students to their classes, now hung in the belfry of Hugh M. Neely Hall, and continued to be rung by the same John Henry, who now had a home on the Southwestern campus, directly behind the new temporary athletic building. The freshmen, just as they had done in Clarksville, donned their straw hats at the suggestion of the student "Sanhedrin," and refused to burn them until Coach Neely's football boys had won at least two important football victories. Mr. and Mrs. Woods Harrison soon made the college dining hall as famed as were the Commons at Clarksville under their superior management. Even President Diehl brought the same green hats and canes, and continued to wear them in Memphis as he had always done in Clarksville, and Professor Townsend became the same familiar figure on the campus, with his cap and green bag always in evidence.

At Clarksville, the home of Dr. and Mrs. Diehl was on the campus hard by Robb Hall, and Mrs. Diehl had been able to make the Robb Hall students feel that her home, and especially the broad side porch adjoining Robb, was really a part of their own dormitory. In Memphis, Dr. and Mrs. Diehl lived in an apartment in Neely Hall, just across from Calvin and Robb, and Mrs. Diehl soon established an out-of-door living room under the shade of the oaks, where she became a familiar figure, reading, sewing, or entertaining the many boys and girls who dropped by to chat and get advice from their favorite hostess. And it was due to Mrs. Diehl that the campus soon became the home of the pink dogwood, the magnolia, the crape myrtle, the iris, the narcissus, the violet, and the numerous other flowers which flourished under her constant care.

Professor Cooper and Professor Strickler were the two Oxford-trained members of the faculty who came from Clarksville to assist Dr. Diehl in building the college at Memphis along the lines of Oxford and Cambridge Universities. Professor A. P. Kelso, of the Philosophy Department, Professor R. W. Hartley, of the Mathematics Department, and Professor M. H. Donaldson of the Economics Department were the new Rhodes Scholars added to the faculty at the beginning of the first session in Memphis; and within the next few years Professor J. H. Davis in History, Professors James Ross and Gordon Siefkin in Economics, Professor David M. Amacker in Political Science, Professor J. H. Wilson in French, Professor R. E. Huston in Modern Languages, Professors R. Penn Warren, W. C. Watkins, W. T. Jones, and C. P. Lee in English, Professors Fritz Caspari and Alexander Boeker in German, and Professor R. F. Davidson in Bible, all former Rhodes Scholars, and all familiar with the Oxford tutorial method of instruction, were added to the faculty.

It is not surprising, therefore, that President Diehl's plan for adapting the Oxford methods to the American way of life met with success; and that gradually the tutorial method of instruction became an important feature in the Southwestern curriculum. In 1931, with a liberal grant received from the Carnegie Corporation for this purpose, the tutorial method was applied to all departments of the college, and a plan worked out which has attracted widespread interest and commendation throughout the educational world. The chief purposes of this plan are the individualizing of instruction, the avoiding of mass production methods in education, and the provision of means whereby a student may go beyond the scope of a class course, both in the kind of work done and in the kinds of interests pursued. The method is that of extensive reading under guidance, and individual conferences with the tutor on the material read.

No tutorial courses were open to freshmen, since their program was largely prescribed. Sophomores might elect a tutorial giving one hour of credit each semester, in addition to the usual five-course program; and a minimum of three hours of directed reading and individual conferences was required. For juniors and seniors, a minimum of eight hours of directed reading in addition to the conference hours was required, and they were given upon successful completion of the work three credits each semester.

The tutorial courses met with approval from the student body. The better students became enthusiastic over the opportunity to read widely in their chosen fields and the personal guidance which their instructor was able to give them when they met with him each week for their individual conferences.

The tutorial courses did not replace the honors courses provided for in the curriculum. Since the honors courses were open only to comparatively few superior students, the tutorial courses served to give a far greater number of students some of the special privileges formerly limited to the honors students, who had received the maximum of individual attention from their major professors, and had been able to devote fully three-fifths of their time in their senior year to their chosen field of study.

Perhaps the most memorable, certainly the most colorful, event connected with the first year of Southwestern at Memphis was the Jubilee and Inaugural Celebration, which took place during the Thanksgiving holidays, November 26-28, 1925. It had been just fifty years since Southwestern Presbyterian University replaced Stewart College as the name of the institution at Clarksville, and it was the first year of Southwestern in its new home at Memphis; consequently, it was decided to celebrate both events in fitting ceremonies at this time.

Thursday, Thanksgiving Day, was set apart as Anniversary and Alumni Day. On that day alumni and friends filled the Second Presbyterian Church to hear Dr. George Summey, former President of the Southwestern Presbyterian University, preach the Jubilee Sermon. The service was presided over by Dr. William Crowe, of St. Louis, who had played such a prominent part in bringing the college to Memphis. Many of the alumni had returned for the Jubilee for the special purpose of greeting their beloved Greek Professor and former Vice-Chancellor of Southwestern, Dr. G. F. Nicolassen, of Atlanta. Dr. Nicolassen made the address at the Jubilee luncheon, held in the college dining hall, after which a football game and class and fraternity reunions followed until the supper served for the alumni brought the group back into Neely Hall, where they were addressed by three prominent alumni, Dr. E. D. McDougall of Jackson, Tennessee, President of the Alumni Asso-

THE OLD BELL
Clarksville, 1849-1925; Memphis, 1925-

FACULTY AND GRADUATING CLASS, 1924

ciation; Dr. M. E. Melvin of Chattanooga; and the Reverend Theodore S. Smylie of Huntington, West Virginia.

Friday, November 27, was set apart as Inaugural and Dedication Day. The inaugural exercises were held in Hardie Auditorium, beginning at ten o'clock in the morning. After devotional exercises, the Honorable Rowlett Paine, Mayor of Memphis, made an address of "Welcome to Southwestern," followed by greetings from President C. Arthur Bruce of the Chamber of Commerce, President W. M. Bostick of the Memphis Pastors' Association, and Superintendent R. L. Jones of the Memphis Public Schools. The response to the addresses of welcome was made on behalf of the Board of Directors by Judge J. T. Fuller, member of the Board from the Synod of Alabama.

Following the exercises in the Auditorium, the audience adjourned to the front campus for the tree-planting ceremony. Under the supervision of Dr. Nicolassen, assisted by Mr. Walker M. Taylor, Past Grand Master of the Masonic Lodge of the State of Tennessee, acorns were planted in memory of each of the Chancellors and Presidents of Southwestern. The acorns used on this occasion were taken from the giant oak standing between Stewart Hall and Castle Hall at Clarksville, a tree which had witnessed all events both great and small during the years of the life of the institution at Clarksville. Acorns were planted for eleven former Chancellors and Presidents, beginning with W. A. Forbes in 1848, President of Montgomery Masonic College, and ending with Dr. Diehl. These acorns were planted in the form of a big "S," to convey, as expressed by President Diehl, "that potentially eternal thing which we call 'life' from the campus of the old to that of the new Southwestern, and . . . to symbolize that spirit of sturdy truth, loyalty, and service, which has characterized those who in years gone by have received their training beneath the shadow of this ancient tree. The planting of these trees as memorials to those who have served as the administrative heads of Southwestern perpetuates an identity and a sentiment which it is desired to pass on through the years to the generations that are to follow."

Following the buffet luncheon served in Neely Hall, the Dedicatory Exercises were held in Palmer Hall, at which time the Palmer Memorial Tablet was unveiled by Dr. S. W. McGill, of Louisville, Kentucky. This was followed by an address on "Benjamin Morgan Palmer, Father of Southwestern," delivered by Dr. W. McF. Alexander, of New Orleans, member of the Board of Directors from the Synod of Louisiana. The formal presentation of the college building was made by Dr. A. B. Curry, Vice-Chairman of the Board of Directors and of the Executive Committee of the college. This building was accepted on behalf of the Board by President Diehl, who delivered an address on "The Ideals of Southwestern." The dedicatory prayer was made by Dr. William S. Lacy, Executive Secretary of Southwestern.

These exercises were followed by an informal reception to delegates and guests, and at eight o'clock in the Ellis Auditorium, Dr. James I. Vance of Nashville, Vice-Chairman of the Board of Directors, delivered an address on "The Necessity for a New Emphasis on Moral Education for the Welfare of the Republic."

Saturday, November 28, was set apart as a day of Greetings and Felicitations. The academic procession formed at the Peabody Hotel and marched through the streets of Memphis to Pantage's Theatre, where Dr. George Lang, former Acting President of Southwestern Presbyterian University, delivered the official welcome to the numerous delegates gathered for the occasion from the representative colleges and universities throughout the United States. The delegates were introduced and presented to President Diehl by Professor R. C. Sommerville, master of ceremonies, at which time messages were delivered by President W. T. Martin of Davidson College, on behalf of the Presbyterian colleges; by Dean George M. Baker of the University of the South on behalf of other denominational colleges; by Professor John M. Mecklin of Dartmouth College on behalf of the independent colleges; and by Chancellor Alfred Hume of the University of Mississippi, on behalf of the state universities.

The degree of Doctor of Laws was conferred on two distinguished alumni of Southwestern, the Reverend Harris E. Kirk of Baltimore, and Professor John M. Mecklin of Dartmouth College, New Hampshire. The degree of Doctor of Literature was conferred on Miss Charl Williams of Memphis and Washington, D. C. The exercises were concluded with the singing of Southwestern's "Alma Mater," followed by the recessional and return of the academic procession to the Peabody Hotel.

Five national fraternities (Pi Kappa Alpha, Alpha Tau Omega, Sigma Alpha Epsilon, Kappa Sigma, and Kappa Alpha) and two national sororities (Chi Omega and Kappa Delta) had established chapters on the campus of Southwestern at Clarksville. During the first session at Memphis these organizations were keenly interested in the announcement of President Diehl on the policy of the college in regard to the building of fraternity and sorority houses on the campus, in which he said:

"It shall be the policy of Southwestern to have a fraternity quadrangle and a sorority quadrangle on opposite sides of the College campus. The College will assign a piece of ground on the campus for each fraternity or sorority, upon which that fraternity or sorority may build a club house of the lodge type, but not a residential house. This ground will he leased to the fraternity or sorority for a definite period. The plans and elevations of these houses must be approved by the architect and the President of the College. The houses are to be of the same Collegiate Gothic type of architecture, to be constructed of the same material as the other buildings, and are to be harmonious with the whole. They are to be erected of rubble stone, which will be supplied at reasonable cost by the College, this stone to be laid in the wall in the same way as it is laid in the other buildings; the same type of metal windows are to be used; and there is to be the same type of roof, that is, the same quality and color of slate. The lodges are to be built in narrow units, of not more than twenty feet span of roof, and the roof is to have a pitch of fifty-two degrees. . . . It shall be the policy of Southwestern thus to make it possible for any fraternity or sorority group to erect a house on the campus, and it shall be the policy of Southwestern itself to erect in the fraternity quadrangle and in the sorority quadrangle a non-fraternity house and a non-sorority house, which shall be a little larger and a little nicer than fraternity houses."

Since the opening of Southwestern in Memphis, the national fraternity, Sigma Nu, and the national sororities, Alpha Omicron Pi, Zeta Tau Alpha, and Delta Delta Delta, have established chapters on the campus, and each of the six fraternities and five sororities represented has built an attractive lodge. The fraternity quadrangle is located in a wooded area on the western side of the campus as it is entered from University Avenue, and the sorority quadrangle is placed on the eastern side of the campus as it is entered from Hein Park.

The athletic policy of Southwestern at Memphis was of particular interest not only to the students of the college but to the alumni and to the citizens of Memphis as well. In the mind of the man of the streets, colleges had come to be ranked almost wholly according to the success of the football teams which they produced, and the tendency of the postwar age was toward "bigger and better" football, and the glorification of athletics and the heroes of the athletic field to the impairment of scholarship and neglect of scholars in the colleges and universities of America. Football coaches were often paid greater salaries than were the presidents of the institutions where they coached, to say nothing of the members of the faculty. Scholarships were often awarded to football players whose scholastic standing was at the foot rather than at the head of their classes; and it was these men who often dominated student life on the campuses and set the standards for the student body to follow.

It was inevitable that tremendous pressure should be brought on President Diehl and the administration to sacrifice the high ideals of scholarship to the desires of the public on whose support the success of the institution must depend. He was firm, however, in his determination that Southwestern would not overemphasize athletics, and at the same time he was sympathetic with those who stressed the importance of sports and physical culture in the training of the well-rounded college man. In stating the athletic policy of Southwestern, he quoted with approval the statement of President Lowell of Harvard that it is worth our while to ask ourselves,

"What is the object for which we are striving in our intercollegiate sports? . . . The two great nations of antiquity whose languages, deeds and thoughts our colleges have always taught, had games publicly attended and attracting wide interest, but conducted on different principles. No people ever set more store by competitive athletic contests than the Greeks; none valued and commemorated success more highly. Their sports attracted large crowds. Yet with them the object was, and always remained, the cultivation of physical excellence in young men. Nothing was allowed to obscure that purpose, everything else was subordinated to it. With the Romans, on the contrary, the primary object was the entertainment of the spectators, the performers becoming more and more professional, while the training of youth in health and strength was lost from sight almost altogether. Is not the Greek principle preferable to the Roman for our colleges? But with our frequent intercollegiate games, with the attracting of huge crowds at short intervals, and continuous publicity, are we not slipping into the Roman attitude of mind? The Greeks thought one great contest of a kind in a year enough to sustain ardor in athletics. May it not be that a single intercollegiate meet in each sport would do the same? Many of the alumni are slipping into the Roman attitude of mind; while the authorities of the university are striving to follow the Greek conception of these things. On the part of the vast majority of alumni, this is quite unconscious. They would undoubtedly, if presented with the alternative, approve of the Greek rather than the Roman attitude in our colleges; but the subject is not presented to them in that way, appearing simply as a matter of gratification in seeing and taking their friends to the game. It may, therefore, be worth while to state the question as it lies in the minds of those responsible for the training of young men."

Fargason Field, consisting of about fifteen acres located on the campus, had been the gift of Mr. John T. Fargason and his sister, Mrs. Mary Fargason Falls, for the purpose of supplying needed playing fields for the use of the students. A modern field house built of wood to serve until a stone building in harmony with the other buildings on the campus could be secured, a football field with temporary grandstands, a baseball diamond, a number of well-located tennis courts, and a cinder track were soon constructed on Fargason Field, and the football field in particular became the scene of many exciting contests during the first decade in the history of Southwestern at Memphis.

"Jess" Neely's well-coached teams were able to score victories over all their opponents except the University of Mississippi and Birmingham-Southern College, in their first year at Fargason Field. Their 31-6 Thanksgiving victory over their city rivals, the West Tennessee Teachers, ended a very satisfactory season. Neely's second year at Memphis proved even more successful when the Southwestern "Lynx" registered victories over Birmingham-Southern, Bethel, West Tennessee Teachers, University of Tennessee Doctors, and scored twenty-seven points against the University of Mississippi in one of the most exciting games ever played on Fargason Field. It was during this season that Mr. Arthur Halle of Memphis showed his great enthusiasm for Southwestern athletics by coming out to Fargason Field and organizing as well as coaching a freshman team, which soon became known as the Southwestern "Bobcats."

Southwestern became a member of the Southern Intercollegiate Athletic Association in 1928. Before the season opened, Coach Neely had resigned to accept a position at the University of Alabama, and Mr. Neely Mallory, famed as "Memphis Bill" when he was All-American halfback at Yale, volunteered his services, sacrificing much time from his business, in order to aid Assistant-Coach Frank Elam in turning out a well-trained football team. Webb Burke, of University of Mississippi fame, became coach in 1929, and his first Southwestern team made themselves heroes by defeating the Sewanee team by the score of 9-0 before the largest crowd ever before assembled on Fargason Field. The following year Sewanee was again defeated by the score of 26-6; and Mississippi State by the score of 14-0.

In 1931 Southwestern became a charter member of the Dixie Conference, and the beloved James R. Haygood succeeded Webb Burke as Southwestern's coach in that year, bringing with him from the University of Alabama John Miller as assistant coach. Their first years of coaching were made memorable by the colorful games in which the University of Mississippi was held to a 6-6 tie, Mississippi State was defeated 6-0, and the powerful University of Chattanooga was held to a 0-0 tie. The first decade in the history of Southwestern football at Memphis came to an end in 1934 with Haygood still as coach; but at the very beginning of the new year the many friends of Mr. Haygood throughout the South were shocked and saddened by the news of his sudden death from a heart attack, which occurred at Little Rock on January 18, 1935. As Athletic Director and Coach, Mr. Haygood had been a regular member of the Southwestern faculty, and President Diehl expressed the opinion of the whole college community when he said: "It will be difficult to find a man who is so richly endowed, who is so fully in accord with our ideals, and who can cooperate so effectively and harmoniously in carrying them out."

At the close of the first decade at Memphis, President Diehl in his report to the Board of Directors of the college could say: "Southwestern has everything save adequate and assured financial support." This decade covered the years of the great world depression, when practically every college and university of the land was faced with serious financial problems. Naturally, the problems of the new Southwestern at Memphis were acute and particularly difficult to solve, and the responsibility for the solution fell chiefly on the shoulders of President Diehl.

Neither the campaign for funds carried on in the Synods nor that carried on in Memphis preliminary to the removal of Southwestern to Memphis had been by any means so successful as had been hoped for. It had been necessary, therefore, for the college to obtain as large a loan as possible in order to complete plans for financing the removal and opening in September, 1925. This fact gave rise to rumors in some quarters that the college was bankrupt, and led to distrust and criticism of President Diehl in the handling of the funds that had been raised. The Synods were wont to attribute their failure to contribute to the assumption that in moving to Memphis the college had become the financial charge of the people of Memphis; and Memphians were likely to reason that although now located in the city of Memphis it was a Presbyterian institution and should be supported by the Presbyterians of the four controlling Synods.

Soon after the opening in Memphis, a special meeting of the Board of Directors was called at the suggestion of Mayor Rowlett Paine and his committee, who had been in charge of the Memphis Campaign. At this meeting Mayor Paine again pledged the support of himself and his committee and stated that they were willing to do everything in their power to provide such funds as might be necessary to keep the institution going. He stated, however, that while Southwestern was an asset to Memphis, it was also a Presbyterian institution, owned and controlled by the Presbyterians in the four co-operating Synods, and should expect its main support from that source. He insisted that there should be raised an endowment fund approximating one and a half million dollars, and said that the four Synods should be expected to provide for all endowment needs. He then requested the Board to pledge itself to see that this was done, stating that if this were done, he and his committee would raise in Memphis funds necessary to cover the deficit in operating expenses for the next three years.

The Board promptly accepted the offer of Mayor Paine and it was mutually agreed that the Board on its part would put on a campaign for an endowment fund of $1,200,000 in the four Synods as soon as the Synods should give their consent. The Mayor and his committee on their part agreed to give Southwestern in the meantime such aid supplementing its annual income as would enable the administration to run a standard college.

ASHNER GATEWAY WITH MEN'S DORMITORIES IN BACKGROUND

Campaigns were duly begun in the Synods and in Memphis, but the results were slow and the outlook often quite discouraging. President Diehl insisted that every effort was being made by the college to economize, but that it would be fatal to economize to the point of making the college a second-class institution. To his critics in the Presbyterian Synods who felt that the building of the new Southwestern on such standards of permanency and excellency amounted to sheer extravagance, Dr. Diehl replied without hesitation:

"We believe that there is no future for any denominational college that is not standard or first-class, and the Church must decide whether it will pay the price, or whether it prefers that its colleges go into other hands. There is such a thing as cheap higher education, but there is no such thing as good higher education (that is, education that is adequate, honest and Christian) that is cheap."

On the removal to Memphis, and in accordance with the amended charter of Southwestern, each of the controlling Synods had selected an outstanding Presbyterian business man of Memphis as the fourth member of its quota of Directors. Some business men are apt to see little difference between the effective methods of financing a college and those of financing a business such as they themselves control. Such a difference in outlook soon led to misunderstandings between the Treasurer of the college and the President of the college over the financial policy to be pursued in the difficult days when the efforts to raise a permanent endowment were meeting with such meager success. The Board, however, gave its support to President Diehl in this controversy, and the Southwestern Alumni Association presented to the Board formal resolutions of "loyalty and devotion to our Alma Mater" which had been adopted by them as follows:

We, the Alumni of Southwestern, at our first opportunity to give public expression to our feelings on these matters, desire to affirm most heartily:

1. Our endorsement of the type of buildings here and our congratulations to those who were wise enough to plan these splendid college buildings and equipment.

2. Our loyalty to the new institution at Memphis, even as when a daughter removes from the old home to locate elsewhere and her mother's love goes with her, so we of the older alumni of Clarksville do follow Southwestern to Memphis with our loyalty and love and we commend her to the later generations to love and cherish her even as we did her mother.

3. We affirm most heartily our love and appreciation of the President of Southwestern. We express our sense of appreciation of his value to the College and to the entire Mississippi Valley. We commend the wisdom he has shown in establishing this institution and in projecting its future. We offer him allegiance and as alumni we call on all sons and daughters of Southwestern to give Southwestern their hearts' allegiance and support.

(Signed) R. A. Bolling
Duncan Martin
Lehman Johnson
Committee

At the meeting of the Board of Directors on November 13, 1928, the Treasurer, Mr. George G. Tayloe of Memphis, handed in his resignation as a member of the Board, and it was reluctantly accepted by that body. Mr. S. M. Nickey of Memphis also resigned from the Board at this time, as did Mr. D. K. Brown of Louisiana. The Synod of Tennessee later elected Mr. T. H. Tutwiler, President of the Memphis Power and Light Company, in place of Mr. Nickey; the Synod of Mississippi elected Mayor Watkins Overton of Memphis in place of Mr. Tayloe; and the Synod of Louisiana elected Mr. Alfred C. Glassell of Shreveport, Louisiana, an alumnus of Southwestern, to succeed Mr. Brown. Mr. A. H. Sarafian of Memphis was secured to succeed Mr. D. W. Gordon as Bursar of the college.

At the meeting of the Board in January, 1929, President Diehl was able to report that "the financial situation of Southwestern is grave, but it is not as acute as it was a year ago. At that time there was danger of the institution having to close." The campaign for funds within the Synods of Alabama, Louisiana, and Mississippi had been very discouraging, but the Synod of Tennessee, with the aid of the oversubscription of Memphis Presbytery, had fully met its quota of $305,000. The gift of $100,000 from Mrs. Hugh M. Neely of Memphis had been the most encouraging event in the financial history of Southwestern since the removal to Memphis. In recognition of this substantial gift, the lovely dining hall was dedicated to the memory of her husband and christened the Hugh M. Neely Hall and a Neely Scholarship fund was established. Appropriate dedicatory exercises of the Hugh M. Neely Hall were held on November 28, 1928, when a memorial tablet was unveiled by Mrs. B. L. Mallory, the niece of the donor, and the presentation address was made by Colonel Neely's nephew, Mr. S. M. Neely of Memphis. Dr. A. B. Curry, Vice-Chairman of the Board, made the acceptance address on behalf of the Board of Directors, and Mr. T. K. Riddick, a long-time friend of Colonel Neely, made a brief address on "Colonel H. M. Neely as a Business Man." The dedicatory prayer and benediction were made by the Reverend A. C. Dudley, pastor of the First Presbyterian Church of Memphis.

Another most encouraging factor during the early years in Memphis was the devotion and work of Dr. A. B. Curry, pastor of the Second Presbyterian Church and Vice-Chairman of the Board of Directors of Southwestern. Under his leadership the Second Presbyterian Church raised in subscriptions to the college more than $75,000, with which the Board was enabled to establish the Curry Chair of Bible at Southwestern, as tribute to the great love and esteem in which Dr. Curry was universally held.

At the meeting of the Board in January, 1930, Dr. Diehl was able to announce that Mr. William R. Craig of New York, a distinguished alumnus of the college, had offered to be one of four who would give $100,000 to Southwestern and that his brother, Mr.

Robert R. Craig of New Orleans, also an alumnus and recently elected a Director of Southwestern, had agreed to match him in his gift; and that Mr. J. T. Lupton of Chattanooga had subscribed $50,000. These larger gifts along with the many smaller subscriptions made it seem possible that the whole mortgage indebtedness of $700,000 might be wiped out within a short time, and the financial future of Southwestern assured. So encouraged was Dr. Diehl by the outlook that he suggested the possibility of conducting a symbolic bond-burning in connection with the commencement exercises the following June. Few others were nearly so optimistic, but under the inspiration and tireless leadership of President Diehl the goal was finally attained, the mortgage indebtedness paid in full, and the symbolic bond-burning ceremony held on July 1, 1930.

At the meeting of the Board in February, 1931, the following tribute to Dr. Diehl was read:

"At this first meeting of the Board of Directors of Southwestern since paying off the great mortgage, it is fitting that the Board express its appreciation of the magnificent work done by President Charles Edward Diehl in building the new College, in administering its affairs, and finally as leader in paying off the mortgage. Is there another man within the four Synods who could have accomplished what Dr. Diehl has done since he was elected President? It took manliness, it took courage, it took faith, it took persistency, it took industry, it took brain with artistic ability and business acumen, it took a heart devoted to Christ our Lord to build, to equip and to pay for Southwestern as it stands today, and that with opposition without and at times within. . . .

"Above the flat memorial stone on the wall [of Sir Christopher Wren's St. Paul's Cathedral] is the most celebrated inscription in the British Empire:

'Lector, si monumentum requiris, circumspice!'

So if you would see what President Diehl has done, look around you! See the splendid buildings in their artistic beauty, built for a thousand years; look upon the faculty gathered by him, second to none in the colleges of the land; look upon the fine student body in ability and in number; look upon the courses of study and the thorough work done. It required a man of vision to do this. He saw, from the old decaying buildings of Clarksville, in vision the new Southwestern as it stands today, and he set out to realize the vision. It was heart-breaking work. He met opposition from Clarksville— an expensive lawsuit followed; he stirred up the men of Memphis to come to his aid with counsel and financial help. With a big campaign, he stirred up the Synods to subscribe the funds. The buildings were started and half completed when collections on the subscriptions almost collapsed. This compelled the mortgage. Dr. Diehl, still undaunted, put on another campaign in the Synods in spite of opposition, with only partial success. Then he interested the Craig brothers and Mr. J. T. Lupton to make their splendid offers. Dr. Diehl started a campaign in the Presbyteries and with the aid of Memphis again, the mortgage was cancelled.

"The Board will not attempt to name all the obstacles that were met and overcome, but hereby expresses its gratitude to our Heavenly Father for the success which has attended our efforts in the educational department of the Kingdom of Christ, our Lord; and also puts on record our appreciation of President Diehl's splendid leadership in founding, building, equipping, maintaining, administering and finally paying for this splendid new Southwestern in the City of Memphis, as the College of the Mississippi Valley."

It was inevitable that the forward-looking policy of Dr. Diehl during the first decade of his administration of the college at Memphis should meet with opposition from some of the more conservative groups within the Southern Presbyterian Church. It was the opposition of these groups that made it so hard to obtain the needed financial support and interest within the controlling Synods during these difficult years. In sympathy with these groups, Dr. W. S. Lacy, who for seven years had been the Executive Secretary of Southwestern, resigned this position in September, 1930. Dr. Lacy's resignation was soon followed by a petition filed with the Board of Directors and signed by the ministers of ten of the Presbyterian churches of Memphis in which it was stated that the President of the College "is not what may be called Sound in the Faith." A memorial from the Presbytery of Central Mississippi was received by the Board in April, 1931, asking the Board "to seriously consider the advisability of retaining as President of the school one who is unacceptable to a large portion of the constituency of the school and of the controlling Synods."

These complaints resulted in two investigations or "trials" of Dr. Diehl; one before the Board of Directors and the other before the Nashville Presbytery of which he is a member, both of which were made at the request of Dr. Diehl himself. In response to the invitation of the Board the ten petitioning ministers of Memphis and Dr. W. S. Lacy met with the Board on February 3, 1931. Mayor Watkins Overton presided and Dr. James I. Vance was asked to conduct the investigation. Dr. J. P. Robertson, spokesman for the petitioners, presented the charges brought against the President. Each petitioner was given full opportunity to make a statement, and to present such proofs as he might have. Dr. Lacy was also invited to talk, and made a lengthy presentation of his views in the matter. Dr. Diehl was then given full opportunity to reply and make such statements as he desired about his views and administration. At a late hour the Board went into executive session. The Special Committee consisting of Drs. Vance, Alexander, Curry, and Graves presented its report, completely exonerating the President. This report was adopted unanimously and signed by every member of the Board.

"In view of his record," the report stated in part, "we feel that the Church owes a tremendous obligation to Dr. Diehl, and that not hearsay, but only the strongest and clearest evidence should be allowed to lodge against such a splendid record. This we have not found in what has been presented to us by Dr. Diehl's critics. On the contrary, we feel that this investigation has not only completely vindicated him from every charge made, but has presented a fresh and convincing demonstration of the vast value of his services to the cause of Christian education."

The memorial from the Central Mississippi Presbytery was referred by the Board at its meeting on May 12, 1931, to a special committee whose report was unanimously adopted by the Board by a rising vote. This report read in part as follows:

"The members of the Board of Directors of Southwestern are not unmindful of the injurious effect of the attacks that have been made upon Southwestern and Dr. Charles E. Diehl, its President.

"By law and agreement of the four controlling Synods, however, the administration of Southwestern is vested in its Board of Directors. The plan of union and the charter state that 'the administration of the affairs of this institution shall be supremely and solely in the hands of the Board of Directors.' This responsibility the Board will not and cannot shirk. The Directors deeply regret the attacks that have been made upon the President. We have the statements of his critics, which are full of inaccuracies. After the fullest and fairest investigation, our confidence in Dr. Diehl remains unshaken, and he has the unanimous and unqualified support of the Directors. His doctrinal views are under investigation by his Presbytery. We await the decision with confidence. His record as President refutes the insinuations and distorted propaganda of his opponents.

"We call on all loyal Presbyterians and friends of the College to rally to its support, and to denounce as false and untrue all statements reflecting on this institution, its management, finances, and success. Everywhere Southwestern is being recognized for its leadership in Christian education. Recently examined by an unbiased authority on College Administration for a large Foundation, the following letter was written by him to the Chairman of the Board, after his official visit to Southwestern in January, 1931:

" 'I have no special interest in Southwestern since I have no connection with the institution or any member of the faculty. I feel, however, that in the interest of fairness I am justified in calling your attention to the fact that, in my opinion, the charges of extravagance that are being brought against President Diehl are without adequate basis. I visited the institution and obtained for the Carnegie Corporation data regarding enrollment and expenditures. These data show that the per capita cost of instruction is low when consideration is given to the high-grade staff the College has. There was no evidence so far as equipment is concerned of extravagance. If one has in mind the buildings, I would say that when consideration is given to the quality of building that has been erected the expenditures are very reasonable.

" 'I am glad to bear this testimony because I was convinced during my visit to the institution that it was doing a fine piece of work.' "

At the stated meeting of Nashville Presbytery held in April, 1931, Dr. Diehl voluntarily appeared, and called the attention of Presbytery to the fact that his orthodoxy had been called in question. Formal charges of unorthodoxy were then filed against Dr. Diehl concerning his views on the inspiration of the sacred Scriptures. A committee was appointed by the Moderator to investigate these charges; and this committee, after a thorough investigation, made its report at the stated fall meeting of the Presbytery which met at the Spring Creek Church, Greenwood, Tennessee, in September, 1931. After a full discussion of the matter, Presbytery gave Dr. ..... a unanimous vote of approval.

This vindication, however, did not end the opposition of all the critics of President Diehl and the Board of Directors, and the last years of the first decade of the college at Memphis were not free from all opposition within the Church. At a meeting of the Mississippi Synod, held in September, 1932, the Synod ignored the agreement entered into by the four Synods in 1924 when the number of Directors selected by each Synod was increased from three to four in order that each Synod might choose a resident of Memphis as its fourth representative on the Board. The agreement further provided that the fourth representative on the Board of Directors should be a Memphis Presbyterian nominated by the Board but elected by the Synod. This Synod at this time refused to elect Watkins Overton who had been nominated by the Board but elected

Mr. W. H. McIntosh, a Presbyterian preacher of Hattiesburg, Mississippi, to succeed Mayor Overton of Memphis as their fourth representative on the Board. The legality of this election was at once questioned by the Board, and at their next meeting on January 31, 1933, they declined to seat Mr. McIntosh on the Board and declared the position of fourth director from Mississippi vacant.

The Synod of Mississippi, at their next meeting in March, 1933, declined to rescind their former action and adopted a resolution which provided that every Director of Southwestern elected by the Synod must subscribe to a "Form of Acceptance" provided by the Synod before his election was made complete. This "Form" among other things bound each Director signing it to "respect and obey the provisions of the Charter of Southwestern as these have been interpreted or in future may be interpreted by the resolution of the Synod of Mississippi." The signing of this paper by members of the Board was made retroactive; and Dr. F. R. Graves, Dr. G. L. Tucker, and Mr. J. D. Duncan, at that time members of the Board from Mississippi, feeling that this paper was unnecessary, unwise, and illegal, and that they could not conscientiously sign it, resigned their positions on the Board. Synod then elected Dr. J. B. Hutton of Jackson, Mr. E. L. Storey of Mt. Olive, and Mr. R. W. Hardy of Pontotoc, all Presbyterian preachers who were not in agreement with the policies of President Diehl and the Board of Directors, to replace Messrs. Graves, Tucker, and Duncan on the Board. Throughout the next decade the Synod of Mississippi was represented by three instead of four men on the Board of Directors.

During the flush years from 1925-1929 the enrollment at Southwestern gradually increased in spite of the efforts of the administration to keep the number of students proportionate to the comparatively small faculty and the limited resources of the college. It was the definite policy of the administration to secure only well-trained men as members of the faculty and to have all classes, freshman as well as advanced classes, taught by these professors. No teaching by student or graduate instructors was allowed. President Diehl was in full sympathy with the statement made by Dr. William

B. Munro of Harvard that "the effectiveness of a college ultimately depends on the quality of its teachers." Said Dr. Diehl:

"The most important thing about a college is its faculty, and Southwestern may well be proud of that select group which constitutes its teaching force. The faculty of Southwestern is as excellent as are its buildings and equipment. A college may be better than its buildings but it can be no better than its faculty."

And again:

"Men of the type that constitute the faculty of Southwestern are exceedingly difficult to secure, for the qualifications for membership on the faculty of Southwestern are unusually high and exacting, and the salary scale is low. The men on the faculty of Southwestern must have sound scholarship, excellent teaching ability, pleasing personality; they must be interested in their students, particularly in their moral welfare, they must have a certain breadth of culture, and, above all, in addition to all these things, they must be genuine and wholehearted in their allegiance to Jesus Christ as their Savior and Lord. . . . One of the ideals of Southwestern is that it is for the best interest of the work to have a comparatively small faculty of well-paid full professors, rather than to have a large faculty composed mainly of assistant professors and instructors, who are serving on a lower salary scale."

On October 24, 1929, came the crash on the New York Stock Exchange, which ushered in the great depression. During the month of October alone, American citizens, it was estimated, lost over forty billion dollars. The slump continued through 1930. Over one thousand banks failed by the end of the year and there were over six million unemployed. In spite of the assurances of President Hoover that prosperity was just around the corner, there was no let-up in 1931. The effect of the depression on the enrollment at Southwestern, as on that of other colleges throughout the land, was immediate. The number of students enrolled in the first year of the depression was somewhat less than in that of the preceding year; and during each successive year there was a slight decline until the session of 1935-36, when the numbers jumped from 386 in the previous session to 497 for the following session.

During the depression years it began to appear altogether possible that Robb, Calvin, and Stewart Halls would be without occupants, and that the Dining Hall, if kept open at all, would have few students to be served. It was in this emergency that President Diehl pressed Professor Cooper into service, sending him throughout the Southern States to place the advantages of Southwestern before the comparatively few students who felt that they were financially able to attend a college where tuition fees were charged. Many of the wealthier Eastern and Southern colleges, at the same time, were increasing greatly the number of scholarships offered to prospective students. For several years Professor Cooper spent the summer vacation in visiting the students in their homes, and the second semester of the school year in visiting the leading preparatory and high schools in the deep South; and as President Diehl reported, it was due in great measure to this arduous work that the enrollment remained around four hundred students during these critical years.

The glory of Southwestern since its beginning had rested chiefly in its faculty. By the end of the first decade of Southwestern at Memphis many of the new members added at the beginning of the decade had become as much a part of Southwestern and as essential to the fame and tradition of the new college as had been the many "grand old men" of the faculty who had added such luster to the college at Clarksville.

Professor W. O. Shewmaker, who could roar loudest at the erring freshman in his Bible classes, and sympathize with him most deeply at all other times; Professor A. P. Kelso, who was as determined to shock his students into thinking for themselves in his Philosophy classes as he was in making "holes in one" on the golf links; Señor Martin Storn, the personification of the Spanish gentleman-scholar; Professor R. W. Hartley, the brilliant mathematician; Professor J. H. Davis, who both spoke and dressed "in the Oxford manner"; Professor A. T. Johnson, who sympathized deeply with all students who found it difficult to get to 8:30 chapel each morning, and inspired them with a love for Chaucer and Spenser as well; Professor P. N. Rhodes, the versatile teacher of Physics; Professor H. J. Bassett, who though small in stature was exceedingly great as a teacher of Latin—all of these had become, along with the professors of longer standing (Professor and Mrs. Townsend, Professors Cooper, Atkinson, MacQueen, Monk, and Strickler) who had come with the college from Clarksville, a traditional part of the Southwestern scene. Late-comers in the decade, Professor Gordon Siefkin of the Political Science Department, Professor R. S. Pond of the Mathematics Department, Professor R. C. Hon of the Economics Department, Professor D. M. Amacker of the Political Science Department, and Professor C. L. Baker of the Biology Department would soon likewise become familiar figures on the Southwestern campus.

IX

Southwestern at Memphis: 1936-1948

THE YEAR 1936 proved a turning point in the history of Southwestern as well as in the history of the American nation; and the
career of President Diehl during his first decade as President of
Southwestern at Memphis and that of President Franklin D. Roosevelt during his first term as President of the United States presented
some rather striking parallels. Both men had been leaders during
the worst depression the world had known in modern times, and
the liberal policies of both men aroused, as was natural, violent
criticism and opposition during the lean years of the transition.

The national elections of 1936 resulted in a landslide for President Roosevelt, in which the people of the United States gave him
one of the most sweeping political endorsements ever given a presidential candidate. Roosevelt's popular majority over that of Governor Alfred Landon was over ten million votes, and the vote in
the electoral college stood 523 to 8 in Roosevelt's favor. The fundamental cause, no doubt, for this result was that the nation felt so
much more secure economically than it had felt when Mr. Roosevelt had first come into office in 1932. Whatever may have been
the criticism of the President, men realized that he had taken over
the government of the nation at one of the darkest periods in its
history and had brought courage to its people, enabling them to
act with renewed strength and vigor. They felt that their homes
had been saved and that the young men and women of the land
had been aided and encouraged under the leadership of President
Roosevelt.

Southwestern emerged from the depression years with the people
of Memphis and the Synods feeling toward President Diehl as did

the people of America toward President Roosevelt. Under his leadership the college had weathered the depression years, and the prospects for the future now seemed bright. Criticism of Southwestern did not altogether cease, but doubts as to the wisdom of the policies of the President were replaced in large measure by recognition of his ability and success as a leader. Two signal honors were bestowed upon Dr. Diehl within the next few years; he was elected Moderator of the General Assembly, the highest honor in the gift of the Southern Presbyterian Church, and he was elected President of the Association of American Colleges, a testimonial to the esteem in which he was held throughout the educational world.

The great increase in the number of students during the session of 1935-36 was evidence that the depression days were over. During the next session the enrollment of regular students passed for the first time the 500 mark, where it continued until the approach of the Second World War.

The establishment of a Department of Music and the bringing to Southwestern of Professor Burnet C. Tuthill as Director of Music, at the beginning of the session of 1935-36, were also evidences that the depression was over and that brighter prospects were in store. Upon the arrival of Professor Tuthill a co-operative plan was worked out with the Memphis College of Music whereby the Southwestern candidate for the A.B. degree, with music as a major, would have courses in applied music at the Memphis College of Music, and all candidates for the B.M. degree at the College of Music would take their required academic subjects at Southwestern. During his first session at Southwestern, Professor Tuthill organized a college band, a college choir, and a college glee club, which at once became important activities in campus life. A small but attractive band house was built and equipped; gay and colorful band uniforms were secured; and the band soon became a major attraction at all the Southwestern football games, and at the numerous parades held by the city on patriotic occasions.

In 1937 Professor Tuthill became Director of the Memphis College of Music as well as Director of Music at Southwestern, and it now became only a matter of time until the College of Music would be absorbed as the Music Department of Southwestern. This actually took place in 1943 when the Board of Directors agreed to accept the offer of the Memphis College of Music to make that college the Music Department of Southwestern, with Southwestern taking over the business and assets of that institution. Southwestern then purchased the spacious Galloway mansion and grounds, occupying an entire city block on Overton Park Avenue, only a short distance from the campus; and on August 1, 1943, the Memphis College of Music moved from its former home on Union Avenue to the Galloway mansion and established itself in its new and beautiful home as the Music Department of Southwestern. Since that date its student and faculty recitals have become an important feature in the musical life of Southwestern and of Memphis. In 1938 Professor Tuthill was made Director of the Memphis Symphony Orchestra. The orchestra had its headquarters in the band house at Southwestern, where its rehearsals were often held; and a number of the Southwestern students and several members of the faculty became members of the orchestra. This position Professor Tuthill still held when at the close of World War II, he was selected by the Government to organize the Fine Arts Department of the United States Army University Centers in England and France.

Perhaps the surest evidence that the depression had passed was the optimism with which President Diehl presented to the Board the need for the adoption of a ten-year program during the session of 1936-37. To carry out this program would require the raising of at least $3,500,000, and yet Dr. Diehl felt that this was now altogether possible. The building needs alone listed by him included a Men's Dormitory, a Women's Dormitory, twelve Faculty houses, a Students' Union, a Library building, a Gymnasium with swimming pool. Said President Diehl before presenting this plan:

"The work of the past year [1936-37] has been accomplished with the largest enrollment in the history of the institution, 502 students, our full quota under the present arrangement. The members of the faculty and staff have cooperated with intelligence, loyalty, and fine spirit. Our friends have responded to our appeals for moral and financial support. . . . Some developments, some changes, and some improvements have been made, but the work has gone steadily forward in accordance with our high moral and intellectual ideals. Every year that passes deepens our conviction that the great need of the world today is for Christian Education, and the further conviction that any education which really merits the descriptive adjective Christian is the foe of all that is shoddy both in education and in character. We believe with Dr. Rufus M. Jones that 'the most important function of education is the discovery of the potential aptitudes in the lives of boys and girls, the training and control of instincts and emotions, the formation of ideals and loyalties, the shaping of the trend of character, and the infusion of life with magnanimous aims and purposes.' "

The plans for launching a campaign for capital funds now began to absorb a great deal of President Diehl's attention. Until such an endowment could be raised, the college must depend for a part of its annual running expenses on the results of a campaign carried on each spring by the citizens of Memphis, and on the contributions provided by the four controlling Synods from their benevolence funds. The annual Southwestern campaigns soon became an important event in the civic life of the city, and the citizens of Memphis contributed liberally each year. The Synods, on the other hand, found it difficult to raise even a fraction of their quotas; and it would seem, therefore, a rather discouraging time for launching a campaign in the Synods with the expectation of raising even a small part of the capital funds needed.

The Treasurer, Mr. T. H. Tutwiler, reported to the Board in December, 1937:

"It has been confidently expected that, with the improved economic conditions prevailing throughout the four Synods, their full proportion of the annual operating deficit would be forthcoming. . . . With its excellent physical plant, its outstanding faculty, its high scholastic standards, and its steadily increasing prestige throughout the country, the future opportunities of the college in the field of Christian higher education seem great; but it cannot hope for a full measure of enduring success without the sustained, wholehearted cooperation of the four Presbyterian Synods which own and control it."

Unfortunately, "the sustained, wholehearted cooperation of the four Presbyterian Synods" was impossible to obtain at this time, and even before an improvement of any note could be made in these conditions a greater national disaster than the First World War loomed to absorb the attention of the American people. In the meantime, President Diehl reported to the Board of Directors at their September meeting in 1938: "The financial situation of Southwestern, always a cause for concern, is more acute than usual," and the Board sent an urgent appeal to the Synods warning them that "sooner or later, if the Church does not give sufficient financial aid, Southwestern must close its doors. And not only do we need your money, we need quite as much your sons and daughters as students."

During 1939 little progress could be made looking to the launching of a campaign for permanent endowment. President Diehl reported at the September meeting of the Board:

"The world-wide social and economic changes which are going forward so rapidly in such a revolutionary way are producing a damaging effect upon our free institutions. The need of our Church Colleges was never greater than it is today, and it is doubtful whether they have ever faced such adverse conditions."

The General Education Board, however, he told the Directors, recognized the necessity for Southwestern's launching a capital fund campaign as soon as possible, and had agreed to provide the salary of Professor Gordon Siefkin, who had given up his teaching duties temporarily in order to help, by personal contacts and planning, to lay the foundations for the campaign.

In 1940 President Diehl reported: "It is gratifying to note that the Synods increased their givings this year, but it still remains true that it is the city of Memphis that deserves our praise for making the continued operation of Southwestern possible." Nothing was reported regarding the launching of the endowment fund campaign.

In 1941, the year of Pearl Harbor, President Diehl reported at the September meeting of the Board:

"No one today, even if he desired to do so, can get away from the anxiety of the present or the uncertainty of the future. Some are asking how we can justify an interest in mere culture when the world is in the throes of a terrific revolution that may even demolish the structure of our civilization, when a cataract of incendiary bombs is falling and burning the homes over our heads. Undoubtedly, the immediate urgent demand is to stop the bombing and put out the fire. . . . Every institution of a free people must devote itself with insistent energy to this imperative task. But none must forget the obligation to the world in that day when the ruthless dictators shall have met their merited doom and human-kind shall turn from the science of war to the art of peace. It is unthinkable that the curse of war shall continue indefinitely or that men and nations shall inevitably be divided into two classes—masters and slaves. Never in all history has brute force gained a lasting victory over intelligence and good will, and we do not believe, despite all the malevolent efforts of our modern Attilas, that the real values of our civilization will be obliterated."

The effect on Southwestern of the brutal attack of the Japanese at Pearl Harbor and America's declaration of war which followed, was immediate. Every able-bodied man in college began at once to make plans for entering the service; and members of the faculty and of the Board of Directors who were young enough to be considered for active service by the Government hastened to offer their services to their country. President Roosevelt issued a statement urging young men to continue their studies in college until called into service; nevertheless, within a few weeks after America's entrance into the war twenty-five Southwestern men withdrew to enter the armed forces and a number of others to enter war industry. Of those men who were left in college, all were making every effort to become enrolled in one of the deferred services. Professor Cooper was appointed by the Armed Forces as representative of the Armed Services at Southwestern; and members of the joint Army-Navy-Marine Corps Board made many visits to the campus for the purpose of enlisting and examining applicants for these services. Of the 260 men enrolled during the session of 1942-43, 181 entered the service during the year, leaving only about 75 men during the latter part of the session.

Southwestern, like many other coeducational colleges of the land, faced the prospect of becoming a college for women for the duration of the war. In February, 1943, however, the Government released a list of those colleges selected for the training of cadets in connection with the Army Specialized Training Program (A.S.T.P.), and Southwestern at Memphis was included on this list. Thus, the first section of the 13th College Training Detachment (Air crew) arrived on the campus March 1, 1943; the few men still remaining in Robb and Calvin Halls were moved across University Avenue into Stewart Hall, and the cadets were comfortably and conveniently quartered in Robb and Calvin, and in several of the fraternity houses, transformed for the occasion.

The diminished faculty, who had already found their teaching load increased by the large number of women who had replaced the men in their classes since the beginning of the war, were now faced with the problem of organizing and teaching the classes demanded by the needs of the cadets. This task was cheerfully undertaken and successfully carried out by the members of the faculty.

The burden of carrying on two institutions at one and the same time fell chiefly on the older members of the faculty, who were determined that the liberal arts program of the college should continue with no diminution of standards in spite of the demands of the war program. Inspired by the leadership of President Diehl, faculty committees met in prolonged sessions in their effort to solve the problems of the uncertain and anxious times. Such men as Professor Theodore M. Greene of Princeton and Professor George A. Works of Chicago were brought to the campus to lead in the serious study of the needs of the curriculum of the liberal arts college. After an extensive study, lengthy findings were made by the faculty on the distinctive functions of the church-related college in relation to the Church, to the State, to higher education, and to the student.

As explained by Dr. Diehl, Southwestern during the war period was engaged in two distinct services: one of the training directly connected with the war effort, and the other of education, broader and deeper in its significance. The cadets constituted one separate group. They lived in separate quarters, met their classes separately, and followed a curriculum which was outlined by the Army. Professor R. W. Hartley and Professor P. N. Rhodes performed the seemingly impossible feat of setting up a schedule of classes for the cadets which did not conflict with the schedule arranged for the civilian students. Each Air crew section was given by the college, during its five-months stay, training in mathematics, physics, geography, history, English, physical education, the fundamentals of military drill, and the elements of flying. The civilian students, on the other hand, followed the usual curriculum of the college, and were not, of course, subject to the military discipline necessarily imposed upon the cadets.

Perhaps the busiest man on the campus during this period was Mr. John A. Rollow, who graduated at Southwestern in the class of 1926, and since the early days in Memphis has been Supervisor of Property at his alma mater. Everyone was impressed with the work accomplished by him; and Dr. Diehl more than once had occasion to call attention to "the superb service of Mr. Rollow, who worked day and night with a remarkable intelligence, efficiency, and cheerfulness." He was a trained air pilot and became, in addition to his other work, a member of the faculty, engaged in the teaching of the cadets.

SCIENCE HALL

From the standpoint of the cadets themselves, the wives of the members of the faculty became the busiest group on the campus, and rendered the most appreciated war service to the cadets during their stay at Southwestern. Under the leadership of Mrs. Diehl and of Mrs. Cooper, then President of the Faculty Women's Club, the members of the Club were tireless in their efforts to make the cadets, gathered from practically every state in the Union, feel at home during their stay at Southwestern at Memphis. For each group, on its arrival, there was held a well-appointed reception in the cloisters of Palmer Hall, or in the lovely Fisher Memorial Gardens. At Christmastime a delightful Christmas party was given with a lighted Christmas tree on which each cadet found a well-filled "stocking" containing an assortment of fresh nuts, candies, and fruits, together with a small leather-covered memorandum book on which was embossed the seal of Southwestern. Each of these stockings had been carefully filled by ladies of the Faculty Women's Club on the day preceding the party.

The members of the Faculty Women's Club were also responsible for the teas and receptions given for the many distinguished visitors to the campus during the war. Great pains were taken by them, at a tea given for Lord and Lady Halifax, to have the tea brewed exactly to the Englishman's taste, only to have the distinguished guests drink with evident enjoyment several cups of American coffee to the neglect of the English tea so painstakingly prepared. They were ready, therefore, on the arrival of Sir William Beveridge, to have him choose coffee at the tea given in his honor, but were again surprised to find the distinguished American Ambassador to Japan, Joseph Grew, preferring tea to coffee at the tea given for him in the cloisters of Palmer Hall.

Pearl Harbor and the exigencies of war time had not caused President Diehl to lose sight of the necessity for Southwestern to raise an endowment fund. At the end of the first year of the war, he reported to the Board of Directors that:

"The past year has been filled with uncertainties and anxieties; it has been characterized by unusual activities and a veritable multitude of changes and re-adjustments. Uncertainties and anxieties have permeated the entire atmosphere of the college—not only the administration, but the students who were confused by all sorts of rumors, as well as by conflicting statements from Washington. In view of the fact that the year 1948 will mark the centennial of this college, it seems highly desirable that we begin to launch a campaign which shall extend over this five-year period, culminating in a centennial celebration. . . . Some will urge that this is not a good time to begin a campaign, and there is much that can be said in support of that point of view, but the fact is that there is never a good time to launch a campaign, and the probability is that later the time will be even less propitious. Courage and faith and determination are efficient campaign directors for a cause which is worthy and needy, for an institution which has proved its ability to meet a fundamental need for the long future."

At the meeting of the Board in February, 1944, President Diehl announced that the General Education Board of New York, noting with approval the program and development of Southwestern, had generously offered the college $500,000 upon condition that $2,000,-000 additional be secured by December, 1946. Approximately $500,000 of this fund, it was announced, would be used to erect a few of the imperatively needed new buildings, and approximately $2,000,000 would be used for endowment. The organization for the campaign was already under way, so President Diehl said, and the campaign itself would begin as speedily as possible. The citizens of Memphis would be asked to contribute $1,000,000 and the other million would be raised outside the city of Memphis through gifts from Church members, alumni, and other friends of the college.

A splendidly organized campaign was well under way in Memphis and the Synods by the spring of 1945 with Mr. T. Walker Lewis, Vice-Chairman of the Board of Directors, as General Chairman of the Campaign Committee. Immediately upon his return from the European war area, Colonel Sidney W. Farnsworth of Memphis, Chairman of the Board, had been made Chairman of the Initial Gifts Committee for the Memphis campaign. Mr. Edmund Orgill, President of the Memphis Chamber of Commerce, and a member of the Executive Committee of Southwestern, was made City-wide Chairman of the Memphis campaign, and on April 22, 1946, the Southwestern "Drive" was opened in Memphis by an exciting dinner meeting held at the Hotel Peabody. The *Commercial Appeal* of the twenty-third reported:

"Sparked by an enthusiasm seldom seen in a civic undertaking, Southwestern's city-wide drive for $1,000,000 got under way last night with the lusty swing of success. A total of 792 workers and guests thronged the main ballroom of the Peabody to set a new all-time high at the hotel for attendance at any campaign meeting. Spurred by the dynamic leadership of Edmund Orgill, city-wide campaign chairman who presided, and the forceful address of Dr. John J. Tigert, nationally known educator, the campaign had become known as a 'crusade' before the meeting was over."

A few days later, on the twenty-ninth of April, the *Commercial Appeal* again reported:

"The third report luncheon for the workers in the Southwestern Pre-Centennial Endowment Fund campaign for $1,000,000 will be held in the Peabody today with Edmund Orgill, city-wide campaign chairman, presiding. The goal is well within sight with contributions of $814,959 reported at the last meeting Friday. At the first report meeting last Thursday $775,270 was pledged."

And on May 8 the *Commercial Appeal* under the headline "Southwestern Over the Top!" said in part: "Southwestern's drive for $1,120,000 in Memphis and Shelby County is over the top. Grand total reported today noon at a cheering meeting of workers at Hotel Peabody was $1,120,033.76."

At the very beginning of the campaign in Memphis in 1945, Southwestern and Memphis had been stunned and saddened by the news that Major Neely Mallory, Treasurer of the college, had been killed in a tragic plane crash in Italy on February 19, 1945. Major

Mallory had served with distinction for more than two years in Italy as Intelligence Officer of the Allied Tactical Air Force. His brilliant "Operations Mallory," of which he was the originator, won for him the Legion of Merit. His return to Memphis had been eagerly anticipated by the Board of Directors of Southwestern in particular, and the news of his death came as a blow from which it would be difficult to recover. In his memory, the Board determined to dedicate a part of the fund to be collected in the Memphis campaign, and to build with this part of the fund a Student Union Building to be known as the William Neely Mallory Memorial Building. Colonel Robert B. Snowden, an intimate friend of Major Mallory, was added to the Campaign Committee of Southwestern at this time, and was made Vice-Chairman of the Memphis Campaign and Chairman of the William Neely Mallory Committee.

When announcing the conditional gift of the General Education Board of the $500,000 in February, 1944, President Diehl stated that since 1931 a total of $325,000 had been received from the General Education Board, the Carnegie Corporation, and other foundations for the library, faculty salaries, research projects, scientific equipment, and fellowships for several members of the faculty. Certainly one of the loveliest gifts received by Southwestern during this period was that made by Mrs. Hubert Fisher of Memphis. Mrs. Fisher gave to the college in 1941 more than 2,500 azaleas and established on the campus as a memorial to her husband the Hubert F. Fisher Memorial Garden, which under her care and supervision has become one of the beauty spots of Memphis. In the midst of the azaleas and among the giant oaks has been placed a logeion; and all commencement exercises of the college have been held there since 1942. Mayor Walter Chandler, who delivered the commencement address in 1947, prefaced his talk on "Challenges of Today" by saying:

"It is a great honor to make an address at Southwestern on Commencement Day, and I appreciate it. Particularly pleasing is the privilege of participating in these exercises in this beautiful garden established in memory of the late Hubert F. Fisher, one of my distinguished predecessors in Congress, and a real gentleman."

The largest single gift received by Southwestern during the decade was that bequeathed specifically for building purposes, by Mrs. Emma Denie Voorhies of Memphis, before her death in 1942. As soon as war restrictions on building were lifted, work was begun on the spacious women's dormitory, made possible by this bequest. This dormitory, modern and complete in every respect, was built east of Palmer Hall and convenient to the lodges on Sorority Row. It contains not only conveniently arranged and well-appointed suites, with bedroom, study, and bath, spacious parlors, recreation rooms, and many other attractions, but also a small but beautiful chapel which is the center of the religious activities of the dormitory. This chapel is known as the Williams Prayer Room and was provided for before her death by Miss Sallie P. Williams, of Nashville, in memory of her father, John Whorton Williams; her mother, Anne Fletcher Williams; and her sister, Susan Fletcher Williams. On August 8, 1946, the Memphis *Press-Scimitar* carried a large picture of the nearly completed dormitory, saying:

"Emma Voorhies Hall, Southwestern's new women's dormitory, is nearing completion. College officials say they hope it will be completed before September 18, when students are supposed to move in. The slate shingle roof is almost complete. Plastering is nearly done. Door frames are up. The building is almost entirely concrete and stone. The architecture is Collegiate Gothic. A new men's dormitory is not nearly so far along."

On September 4, 1946, the *Press-Scimitar* carried a picture of this new men's dormitory under construction, with the comment:

"Southwestern is building a new men's dormitory facing North Parkway and adjoining Calvin Hall on the south. It is the third of the men's dormitories planned when the college moved to Memphis in 1925. In fact, the foundation was poured at that time. Of the same ferruginous sandstone from the college quarry at Bald

Knob, Arkansas, the dormitory is in the Gothic architecture. Completely fireproof, the building has five inches of the stone, two inches of air space for air insulation and six inches of concrete building tile walls. The slate roof will rest on a concrete ceiling. Thirty-eight suites, consisting of a study room and a bedroom, an instructor's suite with two large rooms and a private bath, a large lavatory on each of the three floors, and a social room on the first floor are included in the plans. S. and W. Construction Company are the contractors. Gardner and Howe are structural engineers and Henry C. Hibbs of Nashville, the architect. Cost will be about $150,000."

It was at this time that a munificent gift to the college was made by Mrs. L. G. W. Hood in memory of her brother, the late Gordon White of Nashville. President Diehl announced on the receipt of this gift that the dormitory formerly known as Calvin Hall would be dedicated to the memory of Dr. White, and the name of the building changed from Calvin Hall to the Gordon White Hall.

The end of the war came no nearer solving the problems of the colleges of the land than it did in solving the problems of the national government. Just as the government found that the winning of the peace had brought about more serious problems than the winning of the war, so the colleges found that their problems were increased rather than diminished by the return of the veterans from the far-flung battlefields and by the world conditions following the end of the war.

Southwestern was faced with the problem of replacing those members of the faculty who had been given leave to enter service during the war, for not one of these men returned to Southwestern permanently at the close of the war. President Diehl had, of course, found it difficult to obtain men measuring up to the high standards set by him for members of the faculty while the majority of such men had volunteered for war service; and at the close of the war, competition from those colleges which were able to offer larger salaries and attractive faculty homes made it even more difficult to secure such men. The burden of assisting Dr. Diehl in preserving the ideals of the college rested chiefly on the older members of the faculty on whom he had depended through the years to build up these ideals and who were as insistent as he that these ideals must be preserved. Particularly pressing was the solution of the problem of the war veterans who returned in such numbers, seeking entrance to the colleges whether or not they were prepared to do work at the college level.

President Diehl reported at the end of the first session under peace conditions:

"There was never a dull moment during the session of 1945-46. . . . The past session was characterized by unusual demands, perplexing problems, and strenuous activities. There was Southwestern's Pre-Centennial Building and Endowment Fund Campaign, the erection of two dormitories in a period of strikes, high wages, and shortage of materials. Then there was the necessity for expanding the enrollment of Southwestern by fifty percent, the regretful turning away of several hundred students, the necessity for securing additional members of the faculty, and the difficulty in securing housing facilities for the new faculty members and students, including the veterans. On the whole, however, real progress was made, and there have been some notable academic achievements. . . . Southwestern at Memphis is geared to handle five hundred students. Under present conditions, with a desire to do its utmost for the veterans, Southwestern has temporarily expanded some fifty percent, and will probably have an enrollment in September, 1946, of 750 students. This is the situation after regretfully turning away some three hundred applicants who desired to enter Southwestern. The pressure is great to take in more students than the college can properly handle without impairing its standards and the quality of its work. The peril of bigness is a real peril. It must be recognized that Southwestern's standing in the educational world, a standing which has been won through years of unremitting effort by 'bullheaded' adherence to certain definite ideals and fundamental principles, must be protected and preserved."

One of the academic achievements of the year to which President Diehl referred in this report was the inauguration of the "Man" course. As a result of a critical study of the liberal arts curriculum by the entire faculty, and inspired by the sound counsel and guidance given to the members of the faculty by Professor Theodore M. Greene, of Princeton, on his visits to the Southwestern campus, an integrated course in the Humanities was introduced by them into the Southwestern curriculum in September, 1945. The working out of a syllabus for this course on "Man in the Light of History and Religion" was largely the work of Professor A. P. Kelso, chairman of the committee of five professors (Professors A. P. Kelso and John Osman of the Philosophy Department, Professors W. R. Cooper and J. H. Davis of the History Department, and Professor Laurence Kinney of the Bible Department), who assumed responsibility for the teaching of the course. An effort was made "to work the vast materials of our Western cultural heritage into an ordered whole under the integrating principles of history and religion." A special reading room was set aside and equipped with the books and charts necessary for the "Man" students, who met with their five professors on three days of the week to attend a lecture given by one of these professors, and who met in small conference sections on the other three days each week, with one of the five professors conducting each section. The "Man" course soon became the most widely discussed feature of the Southwestern curriculum. The majority of students found it hard, interesting, and stimulating, although some agreed with the freshman who complained, "If it takes five learned professors to teach this course, I don't see how one poor freshman can be expected to pass it."

Another of the academic achievements referred to by Dr. Diehl was the series of public lectures on "Our American Heritage" presented by the members of the faculty in Hardie Auditorium during the fall and winter months of the year. During the previous session a series of lectures on "The Great Centuries" had been given by these professors, and this series had proven interesting and instructive. Hardie Auditorium was well filled each lecture night; and the demand from the Memphis public that these lectures be continued was responsible for the new series on "Our American Heritage," which also proved interesting and instructive and were likewise well attended.

Perhaps a third "academic achievement" to which President Diehl referred was the stand taken by the administration in regard to football and intercollegiate sports. During the decade preceding the Second World War, Southwestern had gained much prestige in the realm of college football, in spite of the opposition of President Diehl and the administration to subsidized athletics. Coach "Shorty" Propst, of University of Alabama fame, became Director of Athletics and Head Coach at Southwestern on the death of Coach Haygood in 1935. It was during his regime that Conference championships were won and that individual members of the team were given national recognition in the football world. And it was in his regime that the Southwestern football team humbled the great Vanderbilt team of 1936, defeating them on their home grounds by the score of 12 to 0. Southwestern won this game with only twelve men, Coach Propst making only a single substitution throughout the whole game.

Coach Propst was succeeded in 1938 by Ed Kubale, for many years the well-known coach of the "Praying Colonels" of Centre College. Coach Kubale was still the head coach of Southwestern on the outbreak of war in 1941. This event made it necessary for the football schedule arranged for 1942 to be cancelled. Coach Kubale resigned to return to his tobacco farm in Kentucky, and "Chicken" High and "Andy" Edington, other members of the coaching staff, resigned to enter the service. Under the direction of Al Clemens, who now became Director of Physical Education and Athletics at Southwestern, a program of physical hardening in accordance with Army and Navy regulations was inaugurated and made compulsory for all men students. Coach Clemens soon proved the ideal man for carrying out Southwestern's ideals on the playing fields of the college.

With the return of the men students in large numbers after the war, pressure was again brought upon the administration to re-inaugurate intercollegiate football and to strive for bigger and better football squads. Many and cogent arguments could be and were given to prove the value of subsidized football as an advertising scheme, as a means of giving color to the social life of the college, and as a means perhaps of bringing fame and wealth by producing "Bowl" teams, but not one argument could be or was given to show that the academic and moral standards of the college would be raised by subsidized football; nor could it be denied that in practice, participation in intercollegiate football as a member of one of the intercollegiate associations meant to a greater or less extent the sub-sidization of football players.

In March, 1946, the Southwestern Faculty adopted the follow-ing policy in regard to physical education and athletics:

1. That Southwestern decline to join one of the proposed new conferences.

2. That basketball, track, tennis, golf and perhaps some others, be recognized as intercollegiate sports, and carried on as such when it is considered expedient to do so.

3. That a vigorous intramural program be carried on.

4. That football be conducted on a strictly amateur basis, with-out subsidization, and that a few games be scheduled with colleges operating on a similar plan, such contests being con-tingent upon sufficient student interest and the practicability of scheduling.

One of the busiest spots around Southwestern during the war days was the Alumni Office. Every effort was made to keep track of and to serve the alumni who were scattered to the far ends of the earth in the Army, Navy, Marines; in fact, in every branch of the service and in every area of combat. A news sheet appropriately called "The Lynx Chat," containing all the available news of the whereabouts and activities of the alumni in service, as well as the news of the campus, was issued regularly and sent to all alumni in the services. According to the Alumni Office, there were 1,271 Southwestern alumni serving in the war. Of this number 727 were commissioned officers, 67 were doctors, 18 were chaplains, and 16 were Red Cross workers. There were 25 women in this number. Forty of these men and one woman lost their lives in the service of their country.

One of the alumni who lost his life in the South Pacific, in the brave discharge of duty, was William Ireys Hunt, M.D., of Greenville, Mississippi, who graduated in the class of 1934. As a memorial to Captain Hunt his church, the First Presbyterian Church of Greenville, together with other friends of the family, established the beautiful Hunt Gateway, erected at the west entrance to the campus just north of the Frank M. Harris Memorial Building.

The students who entered service at the beginning of the war and returned for the completion of their work after the end of hostilities found that many changes had taken place and many additions had been made to the faculty they had left at Southwestern. Even the official name of the institution had been slightly changed from "Southwestern" to "Southwestern at Memphis."

Professor Felix Gear, of the Bible Department, was now pastor of the Second Presbyterian Church in Memphis; Professor T. E. Hill had resigned to do further graduate work at Harvard; and Professor L. F. Kinney, of the Assembly's Training School at Richmond, was occupying the Curry Chair of Bible at Southwestern. Professor J. H. Kent had become Professor of Latin on the retirement of Professor Bassett, at the close of the 1944-45 session. Professor John Osman was a new member of the Philosophy Department and director of the Evening School, which was revived particularly for the benefit of returning veterans. New men in the English Department were Professors L. G. Locke and J. R. Benish. Professors R. T. Vaughn, James Webb, and M. F. Moose had been added to the Chemistry faculty after the departure of Professors Ogden Baine and J. R. Meadow during the war years. Professor T. M. Lowry, at one time Acting President of Arkansas College, had replaced Professor E. T. Lampson, now a member of the State Department at Washington, in the Department of History; and Professor A. I. Smith had become a member of the Department of Biology. Professor George F. Totten had replaced Professor Wilbur Stout in the Department of Speech and Dramatics. Professor F. M. Wasserman was a newcomer in the Department of German, Professor J. O. Embry in French, and Professor T. A. Schafer in Bible. Miss Olive Westbrooke was teaching Psychology while Professor Atkinson was on leave, and Miss Virginia Moreno and Professor G. D. Southard were assisting Señor Storn with his large Spanish classes. The new position of College Pastor had been established and Professor W. T. Reveley, who also assisted in the Bible Department, was serving in that position. Professor Charles I. Diehl, who had grown up on the Southwestern campus at Clarksville and at Memphis and who had graduated in the class of 1931, had returned to his alma mater as a member of the English faculty. The place of Professor M. E. Porter, who had served in Europe throughout the war, was now filled by the return of Professor Jared E. Wenger as a member of the French Department. Professor Wenger had left Southwestern in 1936 to become a member of the faculty of Princeton University. Professor R. C. Hon, who had been given a leave of absence during the war years, now returned to Southwestern as Professor of Economics; and Professor J. Q. Wolf returned from Johns Hopkins University as Professor of English. Miss June Crutchfield and Mr. James McQuiston, both graduates of Southwestern with High Honors, were assisting in the Departments of History and English respectively.

Mr. C. L. Springfield was still working overtime as Bursar of the college, and Mr. W. D. Howell and Miss Ireys Martin were in their usual places in the business office. Miss Annie Beth Gary, however, was no longer the Registrar, for after many years of efficient service in this position, she had resigned to enter the business world and Mr. Malcolm Evans had taken her place as Registrar of the college. Miss Erma Reese, who had come with the college from Clarksville, was still to be found in the President's office, and Miss Mary Marsh had returned from her service as librarian with the Armed Forces, and was again in charge of the Southwestern Library. The Reverend Roy Davis was now Secretary of Public Relations, with new offices in Hugh M. Neely Hall.

Perhaps the most noticeable changes were in the Dining Hall and College Store. Mrs. M. L. Hill was still in charge of the dining department, and Mr. Leon Powers, who had moved with the college from Clarksville, still presided over the kitchens, but in order that more students could be served in the dining hall, meals were now served cafeteria-style. There was no longer need for the "Lynx Lair," and the whole space on the lower floor of Neely Hall had been converted into the College Store. Mr. William Kelly of the class of 1939 had been placed in charge of the store, and a separate bookstore, with Mrs. Pauline King in charge, now occupied the east end of the old "Lynx Lair." Wiley and Jesse and Richard (known to the students as Vanderbilt) were no longer the faithful servants of the campus; but Herron, who had become the janitor of the Science Building on the day that building was ready for occupancy in 1925, and Tom, who had assumed the cares and responsibilities of John Henry on the death of that faithful servant, were among the first to welcome the returned veterans to the campus.

In April, 1944, President Diehl, having reached the age of retirement, presented to the Executive Committee of the College a letter announcing his proposed resignation. Action on this letter was deferred by the Board of Directors for one year at their meeting held on September 12, 1944. Finally, however, in September, 1945, the Board regretfully accepted the resignation of President Diehl, but deferred his retirement until June 30, 1947. Sometime later a committee of the Board, to which were added Professors MacQueen, Davis, and Cooper of the Southwestern faculty, was appointed to find, if possible, a worthy successor to Dr. Diehl, whose name they might present to the Board for consideration; but by the close of the session in June, 1947, no such man had been found. The Board therefore asked Dr. Diehl to continue as President until a new President had been secured, and to the delight of everyone, Dr. Diehl agreed to this request.

At the close of the year, 1947, Dr. Diehl was able to announce that the campaign for one million dollars within the Synods had been successful. The campaign for one million dollars within the city of Memphis had been successfully completed in April, 1946. The raising of the two million dollars enabled the college to claim the five hundred thousand dollar gift promised by the General Education Board as early as 1944, on condition that two million dollars additional be secured within a specified time. The deadline for completion of the campaign first set by the General Education Board was the thirtieth of December, 1946, but the time was later extended to December 30, 1947. President Diehl could now contemplate with satisfaction the fact that although the total assets of the college when in Clarksville never amounted to as much as five hundred thousand dollars, at the date of his retirement in Memphis the assets would amount to more than five million dollars divided almost equally between endowment and plant and equipment.

As early as the beginning of the decade, President Diehl had been turning his thoughts to the year 1948, which would mark the hundredth birthday of the college. On a number of occasions he had made it a point to remind the Board of Directors of this important date; and in his annual report to the Board in September, 1946, he stated:

"Southwestern at Memphis had its beginning at Clarksville, Tennessee, in 1848, when the Montgomery Masonic College was established there, and the Castle Building, which is still in use on the Clarksville campus, was erected. That institution became Stewart College in 1855, when it was taken over by the Synod of Nashville, which assumed its indebtedness, and it then became a Presbyterian College. In 1875, after the Reconstruction Era, Stewart College was taken over, on the basis of the Plan of Union, by several Synods of the Presbyterian Church, and became Southwestern Presbyterian University. In 1925, with the approval of the Supreme Court of Tennessee, the institution was moved to Memphis and is now known as Southwestern at Memphis. The institution has had an unbroken history since 1848, and it will be proper to consider having a Centennial Celebration in 1948. It is by no means too early to make plans for such a celebration."

At its meeting in February, 1947, the Board of Directors instructed its Chairman to "proceed with plans for the Centennial Celebration in 1948, a celebration which will recognize the services of President Charles E. Diehl, and be the occasion for the formal induction of the new President."

The most outstanding service performed by Dr. Diehl during his more than a quarter of a century as President of Southwestern was his steadfast holding to the high ideals and worthy objectives set by the founders of the college, and his determination to avoid all temptations to compromise, even if closing the doors of the college seemed at times the only alternative. These ideals and objectives were reiterated again and again throughout the years. High academic standards must be maintained by any college claiming to be a Christian college; and every professor must be interested in the moral and spiritual training of his students as well as in their intellectual progress. This did not mean that the faculty should be composed of men trained in theological schools for the purpose of becoming ministers rather than teachers; but it did mean that every member of the faculty should be a Christian gentleman with a love for the Christian Church and possessing the Christian graces that would make his influence felt among the students entrusted to his care; this, of course, in addition to his training as a thorough scholar in his chosen field of study. Perhaps President Diehl was aware of one of the false assumptions sometimes made, that spiritual leadership is a monopoly of the preachers, and that only they make safe teachers of the youth of the land.

One of the objectives of the founders with which President Diehl was in thorough sympathy had been the establishment of a Department of Bible with the same high standards of scholarship as other departments of the college. Every effort was made by him to see that this ideal was realized during his administration. In fact, so insistent had he been that this ideal should be realized, that it seemed to some members of the faculty that his wish was to make this department the head rather than a co-ordinate department of the college.

In expressing the ideals of the founders, Dr. Diehl constantly insisted on the importance of the faculty in making the college. Over and over again we find him preaching to the Board of Directors that "the effectiveness of the college must depend on the quality of its teachers"; that "the most important thing about a college is its faculty"; and that "a college may be better than its material equipment, but it cannot be better than its faculty." By exercising the greatest care in the selection of his faculty, and by his ability to inspire able teachers with his own enthusiasm and his own faith in the great ideals and objectives of the founders of Southwestern, he was able to gather around him a small but outstanding group of Christian scholars of whom he was justly proud.

President Diehl has always been aware of the fact that it is the duty of the college to give to the community the kind of education it needs, but he has agreed with the Chancellor of the University of Chicago that what a community *needs* and what it *wants* are by no means one and the same thing.

Said President Diehl:

"The ideal of Southwestern has been summarized in two words: genuineness and excellence. This ideal, so clearly and completely illustrated in its plant, is the very warp and woof of this institution. . . . Southwestern has always believed in a well-rounded education. It has stood for a liberal education, one that releases the mind from ignorance, prejudice, partisanship; one that emancipates the will, stimulates the imagination, broadens the sympathies, deepens the sense of responsibility, and makes the student a citizen of the world. It has believed that the need of the country is for trained minds. President Lowell, of Harvard, has recently noted four present-day trends in college education: a less vocational objective, a greater correlation of knowledge, a recognition of the principle of self-edu-

VOORHIES HALL

cation, and a stimulation of more vivid intellectual interests. . . . Southwestern is in hearty sympathy with these trends. It seeks today even more intensively to develop the faculties of the student, to build the mind rather than to store it with special knowledge. To help students stand upon their own feet, to direct and stimulate them to think accurately and comprehensively, is not an easy task, but this should be the deliberate purpose of the liberal arts college. Southwestern endeavors to communicate intellectual enthusiasm to as many of its students as possible, to develop in them the capacity to appreciate, along with the power to discriminate, and to crown these gifts, if possible, by the yet higher gift of interpretation. Few entering freshmen come with an ardent thirst for knowledge on any subject. This thirst must be acquired here. The aim of all institutions of higher education should be to achieve self-education under guidance, for the only real education is self-education. It is the constant endeavor of Southwestern to inspire undergraduates with a respect for intellectual pursuits and admiration for intellectual attainment."

Said Chancellor Robert M. Hutchins: "What the world requires is a moral, intellectual, and spiritual revolution; and in this revolution the American Colleges and Universities must lead the way." If the ideals of the founders of Southwestern are as faithfully adhered to in the future as they have been during the administration of President Diehl, there can be no doubt that Southwestern will play a leading role in this moral, intellectual, and spiritual revolution, so greatly needed by the world of today.

Appendix

Plan of Union

(The "Plan of Union" was a series of resolutions formulated in 1873 and adopted by the Synods of Nashville, Memphis, Alabama, Arkansas, Mississippi, and Texas as a basis of co-operation in the reorganization of Stewart College after the Reconstruction Era as the single Presbyterian college for these six Synods. The Synods of Arkansas and Texas subsequently withdrew to maintain colleges within their own boundaries.)

THE COMMISSIONERS of the Synods of Nashville, Memphis, Arkansas, Mississippi, and Alabama (all of them being represented), appointed to confer with reference to their mutual wants in the matter of education, and to mature, if possible, a plan for their cooperation, met in Memphis, on May 8, 1873, and after a harmonious conference, unanimously resolved to present to their respective Synods the following plan for their consideration and adoption:

Resolved 1. That the proposed union of Synods for the furtherance of educational interests is in every way desirable, and that it is practicable to unite in the founding, endowment, support and government, of an institution common to them all.

Resolved 2. The object and scope of the institution shall be not only to train our youth to enter upon one of the learned professions, but also to fit them for the ordinary vocations of life.

To this end it shall be a university in two senses. 1st. It shall offer the largest facilities for thorough culture and for a high standard of graduation; and 2nd. The organization shall be made on the plan of separate and co-ordinate schools, and elective courses.

In connection with every course there shall be a faithful and comprehensive Biblical training, so as to make an intelligent, Scriptural faith the controlling principle in the institution.

Resolved 3. In realizing the proposed object and scope of the institution, the order of development shall be: First, the various liberal studies usually embraced in a college curriculum, and *then* the special scientific and polytechnic schools necessary.

Resolved 4. The sole government of the institution shall be in the hands of a directory, consisting of two members from each Synod, one elected each year after the first, of whom one-half shall constitute a quorum.

With a view to securing the necessary confidential relations between the directory and the faculty, the presiding officer of the institution shall be ex-officio, the presiding officer of the Board of Directors.

Resolved 5. The directory shall, with other duties, have power to elect all members of the faculty or remove for cause, and shall have in charge the raising, preservation, and administration of all monies, either directly or by such executive agency as may seem to them best, and shall be incorporated in the State in which the institution may be located.

Resolved 6. The Board shall proceed at once to secure subscriptions to the amount of $500,000, payable one-fifth down when subscribed, and the remainder in four annual installments; and shall locate, organize and develop the institution as soon as in their judgment it can be done with safety, and to such extent as the means in hand will justify without incurring debt.

Resolved 7. The Synods agreeing to this plan shall at once elect Directors as herein provided, who shall hold their first meeting in the city of Memphis, on the second Tuesday of January, 1874, at seven o'clock p.m., and take in hand the matters committed to their charge.

(Signed) C. A. STILLMAN, *Chairman*   J. B. SHEARER,
          B. M. PALMER,   D. N. KENNEDY,
          T. R. WELCH,   D. H. CUMMINS,
          J. L. WITHERSPOON,   B. M. ESTES,
                                              Commissioners.

(The Reverend A. P. Smith, D.D., and the Reverend E. McNair, Commissioners from Mississippi and Arkansas, not being present, subsequently approved the plan.)

W. E. BOGGS, *Clerk.*

The Seal

THE AMENDED seal of the corporation which was officially adopted September 30, 1924, is as follows:

It is circular in form with two enclosing circles, displaying upon the enclosed field a black shield, representing the shield of faith, having on it a cardinal St. Andrew's cross, representing the Cross of Christ; at the intersection in the center of the shield there is shown the Bible, which is at the heart of the work of this institution. The cardinal and black represent the official college colors. This shield thus divided into four parts contains in each of these four sections a symbol representing a distinct period in the history of this institution.

In the upper section there is a right arm bent at an acute angle, the hand grasping the handle of a mallet, a Masonic emblem which was carved on a tablet on the first building, known as "The Castle," representing the fact that this institution had its beginnings in Clarksville, Tennessee, in 1848, in a Masonic college, fostered by the Grand Lodge of Tennessee, which was known as Montgomery Masonic College.

In the second section, on the left, there is an owl, the Greek symbol of wisdom, typifying the fact that from 1855 to 1875 this institution was known as Stewart College, named for President W. M. Stewart, having become a Presbyterian college under the control of the Synod of Nashville, which at that time was made up of the Presbyterian churches of Middle and East Tennessee, and North Alabama, comprising the five Presbyteries of Nashville, Maury, Knoxville, Holston, and Tuscumbia.

In the third section, on the right, there is the bush that was burned but was not consumed, the Hebrew symbol, sacred to the Presbyterian Church as representing the presence of God, and emblematic of the fact that from 1875 to 1925 the institution was known as Southwestern Presbyterian University, under the control of the Synods of Alabama, Louisiana, Mississippi, and Tennessee, of the Presbyterian Church in the United States.

In the fourth section, at the bottom, is the lotus flower, the Egyptian symbol of immortality, prophetic of the old institution under the same control, but with the new name, Southwestern, and the new location, Memphis.

Under the shield there are intertwined sprigs of oak and laurel, emblematic of strength and victory. Surrounding the shield on the left, the top, and the right sides are the three words, comprising the legend of the old seal, "Truth, Loyalty, Service."

Between the two concentric circles is a dark blue field, a color traditionally associated with Presbyterianism, and the following lettering in gold, "The Seal of Southwestern at Memphis, 1848." The date indicates the year when the institution had its beginnings as Montgomery Masonic College in Clarksville, Tennessee.

Alma Mater

Dear Alma Mater, kind the fate
    That links our lives with thee,
For God's own pow'r that made thee great
    Is the truth that makes us free;
Thy torch has touched our hearts with flame,
    Our yearning souls refined;
Through thee we learn the higher aim
    And train the truer mind.

Thy stalwart towers of solid stone,
    Thy vaulted arches strong,
Inspire our loyal hearts each one
    To fight against the wrong;
Our lives reflect the beauty of
    Thy stately cloister'd halls,
And characters grow genuine
    That grow within thy walls.

O Leader to the larger light,
    Southwestern, 'neath thy wings,
Thy sons in rev'rent love unite
    And each his tribute brings;
And dreams, such dreams as old men dream,
    And visions young men see,
Keep lighted in our hearts the flame
    Once kindled there of thee.

JOHN B. EDWARDS